Compassionate Capitalism:
A Judeo-Christian Value

by

Harold R. Eberle

D1316795

Worldcast Publishing
Yakima, Washington, USA

Compassionate Capitalism: A Judeo-Christian Value

Worldcast Publishing
P.O. Box 10653
Yakima, WA 98909-1653
(509) 248-5837
www.worldcastpublishing.com
office@worldcastpublishing.com

ISBN 978-1-882523-35-1
Cover painting by Benjamin Dar; owned by Felicia Holtzinger;
Cover photo by Jen Dagdagan;
Cover design by Linda Eberle and Sarah Jacobs

Unless otherwise stated, all biblical quotations are taken from the New American Standard Bible © 1977, The Lockman Foundation, La Habra, California 90631.

Credits and Thanks

Several wise and scholarly friends read through the manuscript adding their comments and advice. These include Ted Mangini, Dale Burk, Andrew Breismeister, Rick Johnson and David Bixby. John Garfield deserves special mention as he inspired and prodded me to think deeper and challenge traditions. Tristan Kohl is my final editor and James Bryson is my writing coach. You can thank all of these for helping me to think through the issues and communicate effectively.

Table of Contents

Section II:
Capitalism in the New Testament

Section III:
The Historic Spread
Capitalism and Christianity

Table of Contents

Section IV:
Capitalism at Work Today

Introduction

The principles of capitalism developed as God worked among the Hebrew people in Old Testament times. I will show you this in the pages to follow. However, it is important to note that the capitalism seen in the Bible is not the same as that which we have today. Their form of capitalism went hand-in-hand with social values, including care for the elderly, orphans and widows. God also instilled certain restrictions on capitalism to protect His people from abuses and oppression.

After showing you these truths from the Bible and how they developed historically, I will apply the principles to our modern economy.

When I say capitalism, I am referring to an economic system which allows people to own personal property and benefit from their own labor, wisdom, education and experience. Capitalism is based on the understanding that the individual must accept responsibility for his or her own success. Capitalism also includes the idea that people should be allowed to use that which they have accumulated—their capital—and have it produce more wealth for them. This means that a person who invents a tool should be allowed to use that tool to produce wealth; she should be allowed to build a house and rent that house out to bring in added income; he should also be allowed to run a business and make a profit by organizing and managing a workforce consisting of willing individuals.

Capitalism is the economic system which has allowed individuals to be creative and industrious, thus producing the abundance we see in the modern Western world. It has allowed the human spirit freedom to release its potential, resulting in the advancement of society in almost every area, including agriculture, medicine, manufacturing, transportation, communication and technology. Successful application of capitalistic principles allows a person or a society to advance quickly and even be catapulted ahead of surrounding people groups.

On the negative side, capitalism which is separated from godly values ignores the needs of those unable to care for themselves, such as the disabled, orphans, widows, elderly and mentally ill. Over the course of many years, it can create a huge disparity between the rich and poor. A capitalistic economy can also open the door for greed, leading to the acceleration of the pace at which society moves, eventually entrapping people in a rat race of commercialism and materialism. Finally, unlimited capitalism allows for the unscrupulous person to deplete our resources and destroy the environment.

Strict capitalists would rather not discuss these negatives, but at the other extreme are socialists who focus on these negatives so much that they end up totally rejecting the concept of capitalism as a viable economic system.

What is the proper approach? We must nurture a capitalistic economy but govern it with wisdom. We need to deal with the flaws and abuses of capitalism without squelching initiative, creativity, entrepreneurship and industrialism. People must be allowed the right to life, liberty and the pursuit of happiness. However, society as a whole must apply godly values and carry the responsibility to meet the needs of the helpless.

I write with this goal.

First, I must establish the historic fact that capitalism is part of the Judeo-Christian ethic. Therefore, I will take the first section of this book to show how God worked among the Hebrew people in Old Testament times and mentored them to become prosperous people. In section II we will see the principles of capitalism in the New Testament taught right alongside of godly values. In section III we will study how capitalism was developed and spread with Christianity throughout the Western world. Then in section IV we will examine our modern Western form of capitalism and see how it functions in comparison to socialism.

By socialism, I will be referring to the economic system in which the means of production and distribution are owned, managed and controlled by the government. Socialism is typically discussed in contrast to capitalism, which sees production and distribution owned, managed and controlled by private individuals.

After comparing capitalism and socialism, I will dedicate section V to discuss "compassionate capitalism." I will present this as the best system after which we should structure our economic system and I will be a strong enough advocate for "a revolution in compassionate capitalism."

I am not an economist. I am a Christian teacher who understands history and the development of Western thought. Using that knowledge, I am attempting to offer a Christian perspective of capitalism, socialism and our future. Throughout this writing I will insert examples from my own experiences, having worked extensively in developing nations. People in poorer regions of the world typically live under restrictive economic systems, and hence, it is easy to contrast their situations with our own capitalistic system in the Western world.

I am also writing as a U.S. citizen. My European friends have had different influences upon their worldview. They have also been closer to the conflicts of World War I and II which had strong economic ramifications. Being an American, I write from the perspective of experiencing the bounty and freedom which our economic system has produced.

When I began this study I was a purist capitalist. I saw no wrong in the vigorous economic system which brought great wealth to the Western world. However, the more I studied the more I learned how important it is to govern capitalism wisely and how we must incorporate some values of compassion within our economic system. I am still a strong proponent of a capitalistic economy, but some of my strict capitalistic friends will say I have grown soft and abandoned capitalism in its purist form. They would have wanted me to write a pure defense of capitalism. I have not done that. I have written not to defend a position, but to reveal what I have learned to be truth.

On the other hand, my more socialistic friends may accuse me of still being a cold-hearted capitalist. Sorry if I disappoint you, but this is what I have come to accept as truth: capitalism is a God-given system of economics but it must be governed wisely and applied with godly values.

Section I
God Mentored the Hebrew People to Be Prosperous

God chose Abraham and his descendants to be His people. He entered into a covenant relationship and mentored them to become successful in the earth. He nurtured capitalistic principles among them. Let's see how.

1. God Covenanted with Abraham

God appeared to Abraham and made a covenant with him, saying:

> *"I will bless you...and in you all the families of the earth will be blessed."*
>
> (Gen. 12:2-3)

God's covenant did not consist of mere vacant words. We can read how Abraham became *"very rich in livestock, in silver and in gold"* (Gen. 13:2). But the blessing of God did not stop there. God made His covenant with Abraham, Isaac, Jacob and their descendants (the Hebrews). He said He would be their God and they would be His people. He was not going to abandon them. He promised to choose them from out of all humanity and make Abraham and his descendants a blessing to the whole earth. God entered into a relationship with the Hebrews—a relationship in which He abided with, protected and mentored them.

Some Christians today like to spiritualize the promise spoken to Abraham. They like to imagine that God's promise was merely to bless Abraham and his descendants spiritually but not physically. Of course, the Hebrews were blessed spiritually; in particular, they were the lineage leading to the birth of Jesus, the Messiah. But God promised that His blessing would have tangible, physical results in their lives. In Deuteronomy 28:1-13, we read God's promise that if the people obeyed Him, then His blessing would cause them to rise high above the nations of the earth, to prosper their farms, to give them an abundance of offspring, to cause them to be lenders and not borrowers, and to make them the head and not the tail.

Moses explained to the Hebrews:

> "...it is He [God] *who is giving you power to make wealth, that He may confirm His covenant which He swore to your fathers...*"
>
> (Deut. 8:18)

Notice that the manner in which God was going to confirm His covenant to Abraham, Isaac and Jacob was to give to their descendants *"power to make wealth."* Of course, God blessed the Hebrews in other ways, but make no mistake—a central feature of God's covenant was to enable the Hebrew people to prosper in real monetary ways, resulting in an abundance of possessions and authority in the earth.

2. An Example of Mentoring for Success

Before we go on to see how God mentored Abraham and his descendants, allow me to offer from my own life an example of mentoring someone to become successful.

About 20 years ago I traveled to a remote region of the Philippines where I met a native pastor named Eddie. He was training 16 young people. Most of them lived in his home which was a bamboo hut supported on stilts, surrounded by neighboring huts and rice fields. It was beautiful, but they seemed to own almost nothing by the standards of my own country.

Through the following years of working with Pastor Eddie, we (referring to all of the people working with our ministry) wanted to help him be successful. At first we simply provided financial aid, but soon it became evident that his ministry should be self-supporting and not forever dependent upon our gifts.

One of the first things Pastor Eddie did was purchase a refrigerator. That may sound simple, but being the only refrigerator in the area, it became a central feature of the village. In fact, the pastor divided the inside of the refrigerator into several compartments and rented out the individual compartments to people living in the area. Hence, that refrigerator became a source of income and it was a blessing to the families throughout the region.

Our industrious Filipino pastor experimented with several other businesses, having varying amounts of success. He tried to rent out power tools which we provided, but the tools did not last long in the difficult conditions. The pastor and his students were more successful in operating bicycles and motorcycles as taxis serving the locals. Also, the ownership and operation of a rice mill produced finances for the pastor and his ministry; plus it provided a necessary service to the people throughout the region.

Other ministries joined us in helping the work in the Philippines, but most of the credit belongs to Pastor Eddie. Today, he oversees a two-story Bible Training Center and owns rice fields, a banana orchard, a shrimp farm, a motorcycle, a jitney (a pickup-like vehicle), and many more things which have helped him plant and establish dozens of churches throughout the surrounding villages. In that region, the Christians are the head, not the tail.

In a parallel fashion, God entered into a covenant relationship with Abraham and his descendants with a goal of making them successful. Let's see how God accomplished this.

3. The Concept of One God

The first truth God revealed to Abraham is that there is one God and only one God.

This truth was revolutionary because people during that ancient period believed in many gods. They imagined spirit beings controlling the rain, harvest, war, disease, fertility and everything else in the world which they could not understand or control. The implications of that primitive worldview are difficult for us to imagine today, but try to put yourself into their world. If there are many gods controlling the universe, then this world is unpredictable, tossed to and fro by the whims of those gods. As long as people think that there are many divine beings controlling nature and the circumstances of life, they will always live as victims, trying to please the various gods and never able to rise up and manage this world.

On the other hand, if this world has been set in order by one God, then the world runs according to His laws, and if humans learn those laws, then they can manage this world.[1] So God revealed Himself to Abraham as the only God. He further made it clear to all of Abraham's descendants, *"You shall have no other gods before Me"* (Ex. 20:3). This is perhaps the most fundamental belief of Jewish culture.

We cannot overestimate the significance of this revelation. It was more profound for the advancement of civilization than the discovery of fire or the invention of the wheel. As soon as people came to believe that there is only one God, then they could begin to understand and manage this world.

---

1 For more in-depth teaching on this concept of one God and its implications upon humanity, see my book entitled, *Christianity Unshackled*.

4. A Sense of Identity

A second foundation which God instilled in Abraham and his descendants was a sense of identity. Not only were they selected out of all humanity by God Himself, but they were taught to understand that all people are created in the image of God. No other people group had such a high understanding of the nature of humanity, and there is no more solid a basis for the establishment of human dignity than the Hebraic understanding that people are created in the image of God.

5. A Sense of Purpose and Responsibility

Next in importance was the blessing and commission God placed upon humanity:

> *"Be fruitful and multiply, and fill the earth and subdue it..."*
>
> (Gen. 1:28)

The very purpose of one's existence was fixed by God. People were to be fruitful and rule over the earth.

This understanding went along with the instructions to work six days each week. Each person was expected to tend his or her own garden. People were expected to take responsibility for their own sustenance, provisions and life. Then they were to go beyond personal care and steward the earth.

6. Land Ownership

Next was the importance of land ownership.

God promised to provide Abraham and his descendants a land flowing with milk and honey. This was a blessing in and of itself, but God had long-range plans. He promised to make Abraham's descendants a blessing to all of the families of the earth. A huge step toward this end was to make them land owners.

To see how significant this was, realize that Abraham had been a nomadic sheepherder. Nomads never accumulated great wealth because possessions are a burden making travel difficult. Early people groups who settled and became agricultural societies accumulated more property, including tools, weapons, stockpiles of food, other supplies and works of art. Their homes were more stable, providing better shelter against the elements, and their societies were more developed in the sense of having law and order. The step from a nomadic lifestyle to a settled lifestyle was a huge step toward becoming a people who can bless others.

God had Abraham walk throughout the land of Canaan and He promised Abraham that his descendants would possess everything he could see. God was positioning Abraham and his descendants so their economic system would be founded on the ownership of land—a foundation necessary for capitalism to flourish.

7. Living as Free People

Next in importance was the concept of individual freedom, a concept foreign to the ancient pagan world. Their enslavement was first of all the result of their own superstitions that spirit beings were controlling everything in the universe. Adding to that bondage was slavery and tribalism. Conquered people groups were commonly enslaved by their masters. Tribes were governed with a group consciousness in which tribal chiefs ruled and owned everything. People saw themselves as helpless with no way to improve their personal lot. When various civilizations such as the Egyptian, Babylonian, Greek and Roman became prominent in ancient times, such victimizational thought patterns continued to dominate the masses. Slaves were thought to be slaves by fate. Kings and other rulers accepted their roles as appointments from various gods. People were very fatalistic.

In the mist of that darkness came the biblical revelation that people are created in the image of God. People have a free will. God created people with the ability to make decisions and to take dominion of this earth. People have certain inalienable rights granted them by their Creator.

God had to take the descendants of Abraham down a long, hard road before they could actually live as free individuals. After a severe famine, the early descendants of Abraham found themselves at the mercy of Egyptian masters. Soon all of the Hebrews were living as slaves in Egypt. After 400 years, God heard their cries and sent Moses to lead them out of slavery.

However, it was easier to lead the people out of slavery than it was to get the slavery mind-set out of the people. After they left Egypt they repeatedly longed to go back to Egypt. They discovered that it is easier to be slaves. It is easier to have someone else make decisions. It is easier to not push ahead. It is easier to be full of fear than it is to be full of faith. Slaves submit. They are passive. They obey and they expect to be fed. All of these attitudes are contrary to the understanding that people are created in the image of God with the mandate to govern their own lives and steward the earth.

God did not allow the Hebrews to remain slaves. As they looked to Him, God mentored them as a people. The 40 years they spent in the wilderness was a training period during which time they had to look to God rather than human masters. One generation was so deeply entrenched in the slave mind-set, they constantly grumbled against Moses and God. They did not want to advance. They wanted to return to

Egypt and be slaves. Because they would not change, God let them die in the wilderness.

It was the next generation which God took into the Promised Land. They had never lived as slaves. They had no thoughts of going back to a place which they had never known. They had only one option—move ahead.

A comparable event in more recent history was the Spanish expedition to conquer the Aztec Empire in the 1520s. After landing on the coast of Mexico, General Hernando Cortes had all of his ships burned so his soldiers had only one option: to move ahead and fight.

In similar fashion, God molded a people who would not long for the past. They had no other option than to advance. They had to think as free people. Only when people are free do they advance.

Furthermore, free people work for themselves and their loved ones. They benefit from their own labors. Only when they are free will they be motivated to be creative, work longer and produce more. Only if they are free can they be capitalists.

8. Laws by Which to Govern

God formed the Hebrews into a united people with a common government. As slaves they did not have to hold each other accountable to act in civilized ways, but God knew that before they could occupy the Promised Land successfully, they would have to form a government with laws by which the people could be managed and live together in peace and harmony. The government they formed corresponds with a capitalistic economic system. Allow me to explain.

While the Hebrews wandered in the wilderness for 40 years, God met with Moses on Mount Sinai and gave Moses the laws by which the Hebrews were to govern their lives.

God was fulfilling His promise to Abraham. He was working toward the goal of fashioning a people who would one day be a blessing to every family on earth.

Hebrew government was built on laws with the foundation being the ten commandments. The first commandment was an exhortation to worship the one true God and have no other gods. The second and third commandments demanded that the people reverence that one God and even fear Him (Ex. 20:4-7).

As mentioned earlier, the concept of one God was essential for people to understand and manage this world, but it is also foundational for a successful government and an effective economic system. As Proverbs 9:10 tells us, *"The fear of the Lord is the beginning of wisdom."* Only people who fear God will govern themselves. No amount of governmental control can restrict sin, selfish ambition and rebellion if the people do not first govern themselves. No government or economy will prosper, succeed and continue if God is not at the head.

This is still true today. As our current capitalistic society races ahead, it will veer off course and head to destruction if God is not given the prominent position. Capitalism offers the possibility of catapulting the individual and society ahead, but the direction of that motion is determined by the hearts of the people involved. Hence, the economic system which God developed among the Hebrew people can be used for evil ends if submission to God is not the first commandment.

This is so important that Moses cautioned the people to always remember that it is God who blessed and prospered them. He warned them that after they become successful, they may say in their own hearts, *"My power and the strength of my hand made me this wealth"* (Deut. 8:17). Moses warned them that if they embraced such an attitude, God would let them perish.

9. Rest on the Seventh Day

In giving the laws for the Hebrew people to govern themselves, God included the fourth commandment which says to keep the Sabbath day holy. Let's consider the significance of this in relationship to their economic system.

In the introduction of this book I stated that capitalism leads to the acceleration of society. This has both positive and negative consequences.

To see the positive outcome, observe societies in which people are paralyzed by the lack of opportunity. When the economy does not move, people do not have work, and hence, they lack a reason to get out of bed in the morning. In many poorer regions of the world, men are standing around on the street corners month after month with nothing to do. People seem to act in slow motion, accomplishing very little day after day.

In contrast, aggressive capitalistic economies can sweep people into a flurry of activity. The socialists will point out that the capitalistic economy can trap people in a rat race of competition, commercialism and materialism. Devout capitalists can make the same observation but will describe it more positively, saying that a capitalistic economy can be so liberating that it leads to a lifestyle of opportunities, challenges and fruitfulness; it can be so fun that people are tempted to do it seven days a week and never take a rest.

Checking the grinding ahead of the economic wheels, God told His Old Testament people that six days is enough to work—it is enough! There is incredible power in the assertive act of ceasing all work. This is not necessary in a society where people are already unmotivated to work, but in a capitalistic society people can get so caught up in accumulating wealth, succeeding at business or the excitement of competition that they become totally consumed in their thoughts and desires. The establishment of the Sabbath rest was one of several ways God placed checks on the capitalism He was instilling within Hebrew society.

It is also worth noting how God established seven feasts which the Hebrews were to celebrate each year. These feasts were primarily occasions when the Hebrews gathered as families and celebrated the goodness of God. This had many positive results on Hebrew society, but in reference to an accelerated economy it established a temper of life. Families were required on a regular basis to gather together and have fun. This placed the family's emotional and developmental well-being above the financial success in priority of importance. Resulting attitudes break the momentum which unchecked capitalism can create in society.

10. Honoring Parents

In giving the laws for the Hebrew people to govern themselves, God included the fifth commandment which says to honor one's parents. This honoring offered many benefits to society, but in reference to economic benefits it established family relationships in which parents cared and provided for their children, and then later in life, children cared and provided for their parents. These family ties are one of the single most powerful means by which a society can advance and prosper. People are motivated to work for themselves and their loved ones. Then they pass their accumulated wealth on from one generation to another.

11. Establishment of Personal Property Rights

The eighth commandment says, *"You shall not steal."* It is difficult for modern people to understand how revolutionary this concept was to the Hebrews of that period. Property rights are so much a part of our modern culture that we take them for granted. Yet in ancient times (and among small isolated groups today), people groups often held all things in common. After one person finished using a hatchet and set it down, another person could pick it up and carry it away. No one would have thought anything is wrong or unusual about such activity. This was especially true among slaves and tribal people. Only when we realize this can we comprehend the radical nature of God's commandment which established the rights of individuals to personal possessions.

There are many advantages to a society which values personal property. For one, only when people own their own possession will they be motivated to accumulate more or improve that which they have.

For another example, let me tell you about a third-world country which I recently visited where rebels were controlling a large region and the government had been unable to regain control. Among many devastating consequences, no outside investors were willing to come into that region and risk erecting factories, building roads, installing telephone systems or buying land. Even the locals were fearful of buying homes or planting crops lest their labors be in vain. If the government cannot protect personal property rights, capitalism will not work. Famine and poverty follow down that path.

12. Enjoying the Fruit of One's Own Labors

The tenth commandment exhorts us not to covet our neighbor's house, fields, ox, donkey, or anything that belongs to him (including spouse). Of course, coveting often leads to theft, but there is more than property rights entailed with this commandment.

During several years pastoring a church, I had the opportunity of watching the lives of numerous people and seeing how their daily decisions affected their lives over the course of time. One thing that became clear is that whenever people waste their energy longing for someone else's possessions (or someone else's spouse) they have less energy to care for what they presently have available to them. As a consequence, they do not improve nor enjoy what they presently have. Nor do they focus on the work and blessings right in front of them. In the worse cases, people become obsessed with what they don't possess and what others do. Then they tend to conclude that life is unfair and they are getting a raw deal. Hence, they turn back into victims, slaves rather than free individuals taking life by the reigns and improving their own lives.

The lesson is clear: Don't covet! Stop it! If you want to enjoy the best, focus on what you have. The Bible encourages us to enjoy the fruit of our own labor (e.g., Eccl. 2:24). Only when you enjoy what you have worked for will you experience the greatest blessings.

13. Tithing

At the forefront of the Hebrew economy was sacrificial giving to God. The temple and the altar were the very center of Jewish life. The people brought the first of all their produce to God. This was not a matter of charity or generosity. It was an act of submission and honor. It was a recognition that God is their God and He ruled over their lives. It entailed a bowing within the hearts of God's people acknowledging that He deserves the first and the best.

Most important was the giving of tithes, that is, the giving of ten percent of one's income to God. In addition to tithes, the people gave offerings to God which expressed their love and thanksgiving.

The prophet Malachi explained that the government expects people to pay taxes and those taxes must not be the leftovers or damaged possessions. In like fashion, Malachi explained how God expects the first of one's income. As a master expects to be served and a father expects to be honored, so God expected the Hebrew people to show their submission and express honor to Him (Malachi 1:6-14).

14. Compassion for and Care of the Needy

Another value strongly instilled within Hebrew culture was compassion and care for the widow, orphan and poor. The foundation of this goes back to the Hebrew understanding that all people are created in the image of God and, therefore, worthy of care. This was coupled with the belief that God rewards those who help the needy.

These values were in stark contrast to the values of the ancient pagan religions which offered no motives for charity. The ancient Stoic Greek philosophers taught that it was disrespectful to even associate with the weak or poor. Romans were callous and compassionless toward the needy, values which were reinforced by constant wars, slavery, infanticide and 600 years of watching hundreds of thousands of gladiators mauled or stabbed. The poor, sick, slave and working class were not citizens and, therefore, not worthy of help in the minds of the Greeks and Romans.

Embracing a different set of values, Hebrew society had many ways of making provisions for the needy. First, they were encouraged to give alms to the poor. Also, farmers were instructed to glean their crops only once so that the alien, widow and orphan could freely gather that which was left behind (Deut. 24:19-21). They also had many ways of helping the destitute get a fresh start, such as loaning them money at no interest (Lev. 25:35-38).

15. Holding Each Other Accountable

The principles of capitalism were instilled in the very fabric of Hebrew society. It was simply the way people thought and lived. This included the social values of caring for one's parents, orphans, widows and the poor. These social values were not enforced by the government but there were cultural pressures placed upon each individual to live accordingly.

It is difficult for people living in modern Western cultures to understand how ancient Hebrew communities put pressure on individuals to live according to accepted norms. Conditions were not like they are today where people can live without knowing their neighbors. In their close-knit communities, everyone knew everyone else's business.

Such relationships can be seen by observing communities in third-world countries today. In remote villages most neighbors are relatives. Gardens and orchards grow side-by-side; everyone sells their goods directly to their neighbors or in the open market. If someone is not a contributing member of the community, their products will not be purchased by anyone. Isolation simply is not permitted.

Similarly, in ancient Hebrew society everyone was required to live according to godly values. An especially high value was placed on the honoring of one's parents. Someone who did not take care of their own parents would have been ridiculed or even shunned by the community. The Hebrew people believed they would be blessed by God only if the entire community lived by God's laws. Hence, they kept each other accountable. This was central to their belief system and lifestyle.

As I write this I am aware that this may be a difficult concept for modern people to incorporate into their lives. The idea that we are to hold each other accountable to live according to godly values is not part of our modern way of thinking. We value individual freedom and think it is no one else's business to regulate our lifestyle. Later, we will discuss how Hebraic ethics should or should not be implemented into our modern lives, but here we should note that the Hebrews were their brothers' keepers. They believed God would only bless them if they served God together.

16. Working for All You Eat and Possess

In the wilderness God had supernaturally provided for the daily needs of His covenant people. Every morning there was manna which they could collect for their daily sustenance, but the first day they stepped into the Promised Land the manna stopped falling from heaven. God required the people to begin living off of that which the land produced. From that day forward they had to work.

Not only did they have to work for their food, but they had to battle to occupy the land. In city after city, they had to go to war, defeat the enemy and take possession. God could have chased the occupants out and simply told Abraham's descendents to walk on in, but instead, He required them to fight for every inch given to them. He was with them to give guidance, help and victory, but He was making them into a people who work hard and value that which they possess. He was making them into a people who would be a blessing to all of the earth.

Make no mistake that God created people to work. However, this work was not intended to be a curse or even to be by the sweat of one's brow. God intended people to be fruitful and multiply (Gen. 1:28). He desires to free people and give them *"power to make wealth"* (Deut. 8:18). He wants to give them the desires of their heart. He wants to work with them to help them be successful.

17. Making and Keeping Covenants

Before the Hebrews crossed the Jordan River and entered the Promised Land, God had the leaders circumcise all of the men. This was to renew their covenant with God and with each other. God knew that the people would only succeed with His help and with the loyalty of one another.

God expected the Hebrews to honor their covenant relationships with one another above their own prosperity. We can see this as we note how God assigned specific regions for the various tribes to occupy within the Promised Land, but none were allowed to build homes or settle their own region until they had helped all of their brethren conquer that which was given to them. Further, God warned them not to make any covenants with the people previously living in the land, but to take sole possession without any encumbrances which could jeopardize the ownership and future control of that land.

The lesson is that the keeping of covenants is sacred and must be more important than the increase of personal wealth. Today we can see a godly businessman apply this principle as he fulfills a promise he has made even if it ends up costing him more money than he will make.

18. Limited Government

Once the Hebrews entered the Promised Land, God wanted them to live and govern themselves as free individuals. When they faced national problems He would raise up a judge to organize the people (book of Judges). Each judge was only able to rule because the people willingly accepted his or her leadership. It was, in fact, the earliest form of democracy on a national level for which we have historical records.

Unfortunately, the Hebrew people wanted a king to rule

over them. God spoke through the prophet Samuel, warning the people that if they got a king, then the king would take their sons and daughters to serve in his armies, fields and kitchens. The king would take the best of their fields and vineyards. He would take a tenth of their flocks and would continue taking more and more, until *"you yourselves will become his servants"* (I Sam. 8:17). God did not want the Hebrews to have a king but they insisted on it. They were determined to have someone rule over them. They wanted to be servants rather than free (I Sam. 8).

Among the many detrimental effects of an over-controlling government is the fact that it robs people of the produce of their own labors. It kills personal motivation and entrepreneurship. Whenever government reigns over people rather than serves them, it oppresses the human spirit which was created in the image of God.

God wanted to keep the Hebrews from making this mistake, but they went ahead anyway and got a king to rule over them.

19. Lending Is Blessed, Borrowing Is Cursed

God instructed the Hebrews not to charge interest when they lent money to their fellow countrymen. However, they could charge interest whenever they lent money to non-Hebrews. God even described the ability to lend as a blessing which He would enable them to do when they obeyed His commands:

> *"...you shall lend to many nations, but you shall not borrow. The Lord will make you the head and not the tail, and you only will be above, and you will not be underneath..."*
>
> (Deut. 28:12-13)

Note that being in the position of lending was associated with being the head and being above.

In contrast, God warned the Hebrews that if they did not obey Him;

> *"The alien who is among you shall rise above you higher and higher, but you will go down lower and lower. He shall lend to you, but you will not lend to him; he shall be the head and you will be the tail."*

(Deut. 28:43-44)

Such verses placed the position of borrowing in a very negative light—something to be avoided at all costs.

This was a value strongly instilled within Hebrew culture. They were to be the lenders to foreigners. This was a manifestation and evidence of God's blessing on their lives.

20. Linear Time and Progress

Another concept foundational to Hebrew thought is that time moves in a linear, progressive fashion. This way of thinking was another revolution in thought unique to the ancient Hebrews.

To see this, consider how all ancient people groups developed their culture closely tied to nature, and therefore, they were ever conscious of the natural rhythms of life: how the sun rises and sets each day, the moon repeats its pattern each month, and the seasons of each year repeat over and over again. People are born, they live and then they die. Everything happens over and over again. Even the Greeks and Romans believed that kingdoms come and go; one would rise up, only to be overthrown by another, which would someday be overthrown by another. All things were thought of as trapped in endless cycles.

Yet God broke this cyclical way of thinking by having Moses develop a written, linear record of their history. The first five books of the Bible start with Creation, reporting what happened the first day, then the second day, then the third day... Even the generations are recorded as "this person begat that person, and then that person begat another person...." Few other cultures in the world had written records and fewer still had any sense of progression in their records. The Hebrews were the first to have a written record of their origins laid out as a chronological succession of events.

Further, God gave them promises about their future. Not only would they take possession of the Promised Land, but prophets foretold of days when a Messiah would come. Most importantly, God promised King David that one of his descendents would build a kingdom which would never end (I Chron. 17:12-14). This flew in the face of the pagan idea that kingdoms rise and fall. God told Daniel that His kingdom would continue growing until it filled the whole earth (Dan. 2:35, 44-45). This demanded that the Hebrews envision this world moving in a positive, God-ordained direction.

Hence, the Hebrews developed a consciousness of their past and future. They thought of time as linear with the world moving forward.[2] This way of thinking was revolutionary, and the implications were profound. Let's consider a few implications.

---

2 The Hebrews still maintained an element of cyclic thought in that certain repeated events were seen as united; for example, they understood that when God blessed the seventh day, His blessing was spoken once but it manifested in every seventh day throughout time. This connected all of the Sabbath days in a way that allowed the Hebrews to see themselves entering into a Sabbath rest on the seventh day united with all Hebrew people throughout time who had or ever will rest on the seventh day. Similarly, when they celebrated the feasts, they thought of themselves as united with all others throughout time who have or will celebrate the feasts.

21. Planning for the Future

If things in this world are advancing, rather than cyclic, then people can plan and work for the future.

This way of thinking is so much a part of our modern Western worldview that it is difficult for modern people to understand how much we have advanced and how crippling the primitive cyclical pattern of thought was. To make this clearer, allow me to share an experience I had in a remote region of the world where primitive tribal ways are still influential. Several times I traveled into this one remote region where the dirt roads are extremely rough and underdeveloped. Then one year the government brought in heavy equipment for local people to use to improve the roads. At the time I was excited, thinking that during my next visit the roads would be greatly improved. But to my surprise when I returned one year later almost nothing had been done. When I inquired why, I learned that the government could not get local natives to drive the equipment because they would work for one or two days, earn enough money to live for a week or two, and then quit. Since the native already had enough money to live for a week or two, he had no reason to come back and work another day. He would simply walk off the job and go spend his money. He may come back a month or two later, but again, only to stay for one or two days. Such short-term thinking is common among primitive people whose lifestyle is tied closely to nature.

When God separated the Hebrews from the rest of the world, He mentored them to think in different terms. They became conscious of history and the future. They became conscious of the passing of time.

This linear thinking was evident among the Hebrews even before Moses led them out of Egypt. Consider Joseph, Abraham's grandson. Joseph was wrongly imprisoned, but he was released after interpreting Pharaoh's dream correctly. Joseph knew from the dream that seven years of plenty would come, followed by seven years of famine. In order to prepare for the coming years of famine, Joseph led the Egyptians to store large quantities of food during the years of abundance. This took place at a time in history when most people were very fatalistic, accepting as fact that famines come and famines go. Joseph's wisdom spared the lives of countless Egyptians and allowed him to be elevated to a place of great authority within Pharaoh's kingdom.

Such linear thinking and planning for the future allowed the Hebrew people to understand things in ways which the surrounding people groups did not fully grasp.

22. Inheritances, Frugality and Savings

As the Hebrews became evermore conscious of linear time and things moving ahead, they came to understand the importance of leaving inheritances to the next generation. In fact, the leaving of inheritances became so central to Hebrew thought that it was expected of every person living righteously. As Solomon wrote, *"A good man leaves an inheritance to his children's children"* (Prov. 13:22a). This concept was fixed in their minds by God's act of establishing the Hebrews in their own land with each tribe and family being given their portion. That portion was to be passed on generation after generation.

As people work toward building inheritances which they can pass on, they must be aware of savings. As they become aware of savings they become aware of living frugally. Solomon expressed this well:

Go to the ant, O sluggard,
Observe her ways and be wise,

Which, having no chief,
Officer or ruler,
Prepares her food in the summer
And gathers her provision in the harvest.

(Prov. 6:6-8)

Thoughts of savings and frugality were foreign to the pagans. Since they thought of everything moving in cyclical patterns, there was no reason to save things for the future. Since everything was determined by fate, long range planning was useless. Since they had no concept of capitalism, that is, using what they presently have accumulated to gain more, they saw no reason to accumulate. Frugality was foolish to the pagan mind.

23. A Sense of Capital Separate from Self

All of the features of the Jewish[3] economic system which we have discussed thus far aided in the development of "a sense of capital" which is separate from the individual.

To see this, consider how tribal people and all people living primitive lifestyles orient their primary activities toward providing for their own needs and the needs of their family. They are working for themselves.

In contrast, God planted the Jews in the Promised Land and each family was given a portion of land. That portion was something outside of themselves. It was something they were to take care of and improve. Therefore, their lives were directed by God to be centered on caring for their already accumulated wealth, which is their "capital."

Compare this to two children being raised in two different modern families. One child is put in charge of the family pet.

---

3 From this point on I use the label Jewish rather than Hebrew, because the Southern tribes separated from the Northern tribes between 900 and 950 BC, and then they became known as Jews.

That child is taught to feed and water the animal, along with all of the other responsibilities associated with caring for a pet. As the child develops he will become ever-conscious of the needs of the animal. On the other hand, the child who is never put in charge of anything outside of himself will only be conscious of his own needs.

God put each Jewish family in charge of land and they had to cultivate and care for it. It was their responsibility. It was the orientation of their life. This was a value embraced by the entire Jewish nation. They expected each other to take care of their land. They expected each other to develop their capital.

Too see the significance of this more clearly, consider the often quoted advice, "Instead of giving a person a fish, teach him how to fish." The second—teaching him how to fish—will provide for the person's present and future needs. However, neither being given a fish nor learning how to fish were God's way of dealing with the Jews. He had a third option. God wanted to teach the Jews how to own and manage the fish pond. Then they could charge the fishermen for everything they caught.

This was a huge transition in thought. Even today, people in lower economic conditions tend to orient their lives toward obtaining food, paying their bills and purchasing some desired object for themselves. In contrast, wealthy people tend to orient their lives toward maintaining and increasing their capital. Furthermore, their capital is seen as something separate from themselves. They are in charge of that capital. They are caretakers. That capital will provide for them and then it will continue existing beyond their own lives and be passed on to others.

This attitude towards capital allows the individual to be more detached and able to make less emotional or need-based decisions. It also creates in the owner the understanding that capital can produce. For example, a person who owns a farm can plant crops or have laborers plant crops which may be sold; a person with cash can lend out that cash at interest. The idea that capital is productive changes the orientation of one's life toward the goal of accumulating capital and then making it productive.

In contrast, people locked into poverty have little to no concept of the value of capital. They don't see the need to accumulate it. For many the accumulation of capital seems selfish, greedy and sinful. They tend to feel that something is wrong when they have capital, while the Jews learned to feel bad when they did not have capital. In fact, Jews feel right and even like they are fulfilling God's plan for their life when their capital is increasing.

24. Some Are Wise, Some Are Foolish

All of the economic values important to Jewish culture can be seen throughout the Old Testament, but the book of Proverbs is especially clear. Anyone interested in learning Jewish values and incorporating them into their personal lives would benefit by reading and meditating on the book of Proverbs.

It is there in the book of Proverbs that we learn another fundamental of Hebrew thought. It pertains to the nature of humanity. It is revealed in such verses as the following:

The wise will inherit honor,
But fools display dishonor.

(Prov. 3:35)

Poor is he who works with a negligent hand,
But the hand of the diligent makes rich.

(Prov. 10:4)

There are foolish people and there are wise people. There are lazy people and there are hard-working people.

For us today it is sometimes difficult to admit to this fundamental difference in the character of individuals. We are often trained as children to respect all people, never thinking negatively of anyone. But there comes a time when we must grow up and face reality. Some people are foolish. Some people are lazy.

For this reason capitalism is a better economic system than socialism. Capitalism takes into account the differences in character of individuals. On the other hand, socialism assumes that all people will, given the opportunity, work equally with wisdom and diligence. In reality, many people will not work, even if they are given the opportunity. When they do not work, it is unjust to expect the diligent and wise to carry all of the responsibility. That is why socialism has never worked. It is unjust. It is built on the false assumption that people are all equally wise and diligent. Socialism is built on a lie concerning the nature of humanity. In contrast, capitalism is built on the truth of human nature. It recognizes people's individuality and it justly rewards those who use wisdom and work diligently.

25. God's People Should Prosper!

Finally, we can note that the Jews *expected to prosper*. They believed that the wise and diligent should advance above and beyond those who are foolish and lazy. They believed that their culture was God-inspired, and therefore, superior to others. They believed that if they lived according to God's ways they would excel above the surrounding people groups. They also believed that they should advance because they are God's people with His blessings on their lives.

This too is a difficult concept for many modern people to

accept. We are taught not to be arrogant nor think of our lifestyle as superior to others. Yet, those who believe the Bible will recognize God's hand in developing the Jewish economic system. Therefore, they will believe that the diligent application of capitalistic principles will bring blessings. They will expect to prosper above other people who do not live by biblical principles.

The impact of this way of thinking upon Jewish life must not be minimized. The belief that their way of living is, at best, God inspired and, at worst, better than others' ways has been a source of strength for Jews throughout history. It has also been a source of heartache. That belief has allowed the Jews to advance, but non-Jewish people have often looked upon the Jewish sense of confidence as arrogance. Throughout history, Gentiles have recognized how the Jews have repeatedly risen to the top even when they were put at political and financial disadvantages. They have been persecuted for their tendency to succeed but in spite of that, they have indeed prospered.

Summary

As Christians, we value the foundation of the ancient Hebrew people because it was developed as they related to God. It was under His mentoring that their laws and traditions were molded. It was under His guidance that the principles of capitalism were developed.

Those values included:

1) Belief in one God,
2) Sense of identity,
3) Sense of purpose and responsibility to manage themselves and the earth
4) Individual freedom,
5) Importance of land ownership,
6) Government established on the Ten Commandments,
7) Fear of and reverence for God,
8) Resting one day each week,
9) Strong parent/children relationships,
10) Ownership of personal property,
11) Enjoying the fruit of one's own labors,
12) Giving tithes and offerings,
13) Care for the orphans, widows and poor,
14) Holding each other accountable,
15) Working for all one eats and possesses,
16) Making and keeping covenants,
17) Limited government (although they did not learn this lesson very well),
18) Lending is blessed, borrowing is cursed,
19) Time is linear, society is advancing,
20) Planning for the future,
21) Leaving an inheritance for one's descendants,
22) Frugality and savings,

23) Developing a sense of capital separate from self,
24) Understanding that
      some people are wise and some are foolish,
      some people are diligent and some are lazy,
25) Knowing that God's people should prosper.

To summarize we can say that God developed the fundamentals of a capitalistic society among the Jews. However, application of the principles of capitalism were united with social values. Jewish culture was saturated with thoughts of submitting to God by giving tithes and offerings, along with the care of one's family and compassion for the poor. There were also expectations and demands placed upon the individual capitalist. Those expectations and demands were not enforced by the government, but they were enforced by community pressures. People could not live selfishly accumulating wealth with no regard for those around them. They were allowed and expected to prosper according to their own labors, but they had to be a contributing member of their community.

Section II
Capitalism in the
New Testament

The first Christians were Jews. They held values founded in the Jewish culture and the Old Testament. The writings of the New Testament reflect those values. Let's take a look.

26. The First Christians Were Capitalists

In the book of Acts we can read how the new believers living in Jerusalem sold their possessions and then gave the proceeds to help other believers. From this report, some people conclude that we should all sell everything we own and hold all things in common. Some even conclude that God must have been a capitalist in the Old Testament and a socialist in the New Testament. A more careful reading reveals something very different.

It is true that the early believers sold their possessions:

> *and they began selling their possessions and were sharing them with all, as anyone might have need.*
> (Acts 2:45)

Note, they "began" selling; they did not sell everything. The very next verse puts things in perspective:

> *Day by day continuing with one mind in the temple, breaking bread from house to house ...*
> (Acts 2:46)

From this we can conclude that they did not sell all of their houses—in fact, they continued meeting in their homes.

Yes, God stirred within the hearts of the first believers a love which caused them to share with one another. This leads us to conclude that love for others and obedience to God is of higher priority than the accumulation of personal wealth. However, we must not miss the fact that those first disciples were living as capitalists who accumulated wealth, including homes for themselves and extra homes. Plus, they could freely sell their own properties and use the proceeds however they desired.

It is also important to understand the historical setting in which those first century believers were living. During those first few years many Christians were driven out of Jerusalem due to tremendous persecution. Worse yet, Jerusalem was completely destroyed by the Romans in 70 AD, so all of those believers were going to lose their properties anyway. A modern capitalist will point out that God inspired those Christians to sell their homes right before the market collapsed.

The fact that the early Christians sold their possessions does not tell us they were socialists. To the contrary, they were capitalists motivated by love and led by the Spirit of God.

27. New Testament Capitalism

If we take a close look at the New Testament we find clear teachings which reflect capitalistic values.

Consider the parable Jesus told of a master who entrusted his three servants with various amounts of wealth (Matt. 25:14-30). The first servant was entrusted with five talents, the second servant with two talents, and the third with one talent (a talent was about $1,000 in silver content, much more in buying power). The master of those servants told them to do business with the money while he traveled off to a distant region. Jesus explained that while the master was away, *"the one who had received the five talents went and traded with them, and gained five more talents"* (vs. 16). The servant who received two talents also went and traded, turning his two talents into four. The third servant who only received one talent, dug a hole and hid his talent.

Jesus went on to explain how the master of those servants eventually returned and then demanded each servant to give an accounting of the talents with which he was entrusted. The first and second servants who traded with their talents were praised, while the third servant was rebuked by his master:

> *"You wicked lazy slave...you ought to* [at the very least] *have put money in the bank, and on my arrival I would have received my money back with interest."*
>
> (vs. 26)

There are several capitalistic principles evident in this parable. First, the slaves were put in charge of capital which was separate from self. Second, they were told to do business and invest that capital. Third, putting money in the bank in order to receive interest was put in a positive light (but not as positive as increasing money through business and trade). Fourth, Jesus expressed the Jewish understanding of human nature: there are wise people and there are foolish people; there are hard-working people and there are lazy people. Everyone should be rewarded accordingly.

Jesus went on to explain how the men who traded their talents wisely and diligently were given more, while the talent of the lazy slave was taken away. Jesus explained:

> *"For to everyone who has, more shall be given, and*

> *he will have an abundance; but from the one who*
> *does not have, even what he does have shall be*
> *taken away."*

(Matt. 25:29)

"To have" something, in the sense spoken of here, is to take responsibility for it, and hence, to trade or invest it as the two faithful servants did. In contrast, the one servant did not "have his talent" in the sense of ownership, willing to take responsibility for it.

Jesus said that whoever has shall be given more, and whoever does not have shall lose what he has. This is the opposite of what socialism dictates. Someone with socialistic values would think that the government should take away from him who has more and give it to the one who has less. Jesus explained that life isn't like that. To whomever has shall more be given. That is the way God works. Of course, God is Jehovah-jireh and He will be a Provider for anyone, but He will only bless abundantly those who take responsibility for the possessions they have already obtained.

28. Caring for the Needy

Alongside the capitalistic principles found in the New Testament, there is also a strong emphasis on caring for the less fortunate. Right after the parable of the talents which we just discussed, Jesus went on to describe judgment day when the sheep will be separated to His right and the goats to His left.

> *"Then the King will say to those on His right,*
> *'Come, you who are blessed of my Father, inherit*
> *the kingdom prepared for you from the founda-*
> *tion of the world. For I was hungry, and you gave*

Me something to eat; I was thirsty, and you gave Me something to drink; I was a stranger, and you invited me in; naked, and you clothed Me; I was sick, and you visited Me; I was in prison, and you came to Me.'"

(Matt. 25:34-36)

Jesus went on to explain, *"to the extent you did it to one of these brothers of Mine, even the least of them, you did it to Me"* (Matt. 25:40).

There are other passages in which Jesus associated judgment with how we care for the needy. One of the most profound is the parable He told of a rich man and Lazarus (Luke 16:19-31). The rich man lived an opulent lifestyle while Lazarus longed to eat the crumbs falling from the rich man's table. Jesus explained that after the two died, Lazarus was taken to a place of blessing and the rich man suffered in a place of torment.

Such passages clearly reveal the importance of using that which we have to help others. This was reinforced by the lifestyle of our Lord, who directed much of His own ministry toward the needy. He came to preach good news to the poor and set free those who are oppressed (Luke 4:18). Jesus associated with the downtrodden and lowly. He revealed the heart of God and established a pattern by which all Christians should live.

It is also important to note the blessings associated with helping the poor. Not only in the next life, but God has promised to bless in this life those who care for the needy.

29. He Who Has Ears to Hear, Let Him Hear

Before we go on to see other godly values which should be taught right alongside of capitalistic principles, it would be helpful to consider our own receptivity to hearing these truths. Some purist capitalists may want to hear the New Testament verses which support capitalistic principles without hearing those which talk about our social responsibilities toward others. On the other hand, some purist socialists may want to focus only on the passages which reveal our social responsibilities.

That reveals the problem we so often face whenever there are two sides to an issue. People choose to only focus on the information which supports their already held beliefs. Hence, no one is listening. No one is learning. No one is growing.

The same Lord who said, *"to everyone who has, more shall be given,"* also said, *"to the extent you did it to one of these brothers of Mine, even the least of them, you did it to Me."*

The New Testament not only places strong moral values on compassion for the needy, but it also gives warnings about the dangers of accumulating great wealth. There are some Christian groups which so emphasize these warnings that they put fear in the listeners and kill entrepreneurialism. At the other extreme are Christians who completely avoid discussing or even reading the warnings. The truth will set us free of either extreme.

30. Futility of Hoarding Great Wealth

When a certain man asked Jesus to tell his brother to give him his share of his family inheritance, Jesus cautioned the man about his attitude:

> *"not even when one has an abundance does his life consist of his possessions."*
>
> (Luke 12:15b)

Jesus went on and told of a rich man who's land was very

productive so the rich man decided to tear down his present barns and build bigger ones to store all of his grain and goods. After the man reassured himself that he was wealthy and now he could *"eat, drink and be merry,"* God said to him:

> *You fool! This very night your soul is required of you; and now who will own what you have prepared?*
>
> (Luke 12:20)

Jesus summarized the parable saying, *"So is the man who stores up treasure for himself, and is not rich toward God"* (Luke 12:21).

A disciple of Jesus must not loose sight of the transitory nature of possessions. Spending one's life trying to accumulate great amounts of wealth is vain and futile. Furthermore, there is an actual danger in storing up great wealth. Jesus cautioned, *"where your treasure is, there your heart will be also."* Jesus was warning of the luring power of wealth. It is a warning not to be taken lightly.

31. Avoiding Greed

Another New Testament value which must be linked to the principles of capitalism is the avoidance of greed. Jesus rebuked the Pharisees as being *"full of greed and self-indulgence"* (Matt. 23:25 NIV). Further, they were described as *"lovers of money"* (Luke 16:14).

In Mark 4:1-8, Jesus told the parable of the sower and the seeds; then He explained that seeds sown among the thorns represent the individuals:

> *"who have heard the word, but the worries of the world, and the deceitfulness of riches, and the*

> *desires for other things enter in and choke the word and it becomes unfruitful.*"
>
> (Mark 4:18b-19)

Riches can be deceptive. They can render a person unable to respond to the will of God.

Deception by definition means the victim does not know he or she is being deceived. The individual can be subtly drawn away and down a course of life contrary to the will of God.

This concept of the *"deceitfulness of riches"* is seen in other passages as well. Paul warned:

> *But those who want to get rich fall into temptation and a snare and many foolish and harmful desires which plunge men into ruin and destruction.*
>
> (I Tim. 6:9)

The desire to become rich can cause one to veer off course and head in a direction ending in ruin.

32. Applying Contrary Principles

At first glance these cautions concerning seeking wealth may seem diametrically opposed to capitalism. This is because capitalism entails the pursuit of wealth while these New Testament warnings seem to discourage it. How are we to put these two directives together?

It is important to understand that the truths of the New Testament must be understood in the framework laid down in the Old Testament. The New Testament does not eliminate the teachings of the Old. Rather it builds on the Old Testament. The Jews were already founded in capitalistic principles. They were industrious. They believed God wanted them to be blessed.

However, their capitalistic lifestyles opened the door for certain dangers. God was not trying to hinder them from being capitalistic. He was cautioning them about its dangers. To see this, we can compare capitalism to driving an automobile. A person may travel fast and great distances by driving a car, however if one is careless they can harm others or easily end up in the ditch. Similarly, application of capitalistic principles will greatly facilitate the accumulation of wealth, however, there are dangers involved for self and others.

33. Work to Care for Self and Family

Having noted the dangers of pursuing wealth, it is worth noting again the biblical foundation of capitalism. The apostle Paul made in clear:

> *If anyone is not willing to work, then he is not to eat, either.*
>
> (II Thess. 3:10b)

> *But if anyone does not provide for his own, and especially for those of his household, he has denied the faith and is worse than an unbeliever.*
>
> (I Tim. 5:8)

The message is clear. Work for what you eat and possess. Provide for your family.

34. Advancement and Progress

In addition to the ethic of hard work, the New Testament reaffirms the Jewish concept of linear time and progress. This becomes even more well established by the central teaching about God's kingdom. Jesus came preaching that the kingdom of God is at hand, meaning it was within reach and available. He further told parables of the kingdom growing like seeds in the soil or yeast in dough—the point being that the kingdom is growing in the earth and it will continue to grow until it fills the earth.

As people pray, *"Thy kingdom come, Thy will be done on earth..."* they are reaffirming the fundamental Christian belief that the kingdom of God is increasing on earth. This means that the governance of God is increasing. God is directing this world toward His ultimate aim wherein Jesus will rule over all. This understanding is not only central in the New Testament but it has been a foundation for Christian thought throughout Church history. All things are moving in the direction of God's ultimate goals.

35. Financing the Gospel

Finally, we should note that there is one financial principle in the New Testament which is not evident in the Old Testament. When Jesus commissioned His disciples to go and preach the gospel around the world, He implied that this was the responsibility of the whole Church. The apostle Paul confirmed this as he exhorted people to give financially toward the preaching of the gospel.

Summary

The New Testament is built on the truths laid down in the Old Testament. It reaffirms the fundamentals of capitalism, but Jesus adds warnings about the dangers of greed and accumulating great wealth. He also refocuses people on their responsibilities to care for the needy, destitute and imprisoned. The orientation of His own life to help the outcasts of society also calls us to orient our lives accordingly. Finally, He calls us all to further the spread of His message and His will throughout the earth.

Section III
The Historic Spread of Capitalism and Christianity

The first Christians were Jews holding to the fundamental principles of capitalism, however, the corresponding values did not quickly spread to the rest of the world. In fact, Christianity lost touch with its Jewish roots as it spread into the Roman Empire. It was not until the twelfth century that capitalism began to re-emerge, first among European Christians and then spreading to most of the Western world. Let's follow the advancement of history to see this.

36. A Realistic View of the Ancient Period

Many modern historians depict the advancement of Western civilization with an anti-Christian bias. They typically start off praising the ancient Greco-Roman period (ca. B.C. 332-A.D. 400) as a golden age. Then they go on to denounce the Middle Ages (ca. A.D. 400-1500) when Christianity was spreading into Europe as a period of ignorance, oppression and great suffering. Many Westerners have been so indoctrinated into this view of history that they have a difficult time shaking free of its underling bias.

Historians with more integrity speak about the actual depravity and suffering evident throughout the Greek and Roman Empires. Concerning that period Ernest Hampden Cook wrote:

> Few people in these days have an adequate conception of the misery and degradation which were then the common lot of almost all mankind, owing to the monstrous wickedness of the times, to

continual war, to the cruelties of political despotism, and of everywhere-prevailing slavery.[4]

Among the masses in the Roman and Greek empires, starvation, famines and plagues were commonplace. At the birth of Christ over 40 percent of the people in Italy were slaves and the common people did not live much better than slaves.

When the first century Christians migrated out of the land of Israel, they came face to face with the Greek and Roman people. The value system of the Greeks and Romans was very different than their own. First of all, the Greeks and Romans believed in many gods, and second, they had no concept of the dignity of man.

Roman citizens considered themselves free, but this was in the midst of masses of slaves doing most of the labor. A person was valued only if he or she could contribute to the State. Greek philosophers like Plato and Aristotle wrote how all manual labor should be done by slaves, and slaves were thought to be slaves by fate, being inferior to free men. Further, the Greeks and Romans had no concept of labor or commerce being a virtuous activity. The great Roman thinker, Cicero, wrote that "there is nothing noble about a workshop."[5] Aristotle said, "...citizens should not live a vulgar or a merchant's way of life, for this sort of life is ignoble and contrary to virtue."[6] The privileged elite would never bow so low as to do manual labor or engage in commerce.

Modern people sometimes longingly imagine living back in ancient Rome or Greece. They imagine walking upon the carefully laid stones forming the streets of Rome. They think of the thrill and grandeur of 50,000 people roaring in the

---

4 Earnest Hampton Cook, *The Christ Has Come*, 1895, p. xvi.

5 V. Gordon Chide, *The Cambridge Economic History of Europe*, vol. 2 (Cambridge: Cambridge University Press, 1952), p. 53.

6 Reeve, C.D.C. trans. *Aristotle Politics* (Cambridge: Hackett Publishing Company, 1998) VII, 1328 b. 40.

Roman Colosseum. They think of the proud Roman citizens, feasting at their tables and dining with wealthy guests.

In reality, such idolized images can only be formed if people are thinking of themselves living in the top two percent of Roman society and, at the same time, ignoring the masses who were suffering in unimaginable ways. Take another view of the Colosseum and think what lies behind those 50,000 seats. The Colosseum was funded with the wealth taken from Jerusalem when over one millions Jews were slaughter in 70 AD. It was built on the backs of uncounted numbers of slaves imported from conquered nations. In that Colosseum hundreds of thousands of wild animals mauled and killed each other. Tens of thousands of gladiators fought to the death. Millions of people (a large percent being Christians) were tortured and brutally murdered before cheering crowds. The name "Colosseum" was derived from the Colossus Neronis, a nearby statue which Nero had erected of himself so people could revere him as god. To a modern observer such an image should reveal the depravity of the Roman mind and provide a glimpse at what the rest of the Empire must have been like.

37. Christianity Spreading into Europe

For over 250 years Christians were persecuted and survived only as a sect within the Roman empire. Then in the year 313, Constantine legalized Christianity and soon it became the dominant religion of the empire. When the city of Rome was sacked in 410, Christianity emerged as the largest most coherent group. From that time forward the Church in Rome gradually increased its influence over Europe, thus ushering in the Middle Ages (ca. A.D. 400-1500).

As mentioned earlier, historians who are antagonistic toward Christianity like to put the Middle Ages in a very bad light. They like to label the early part of the period as the

Dark Ages (ca. A.D. 400-1000), with all of the implications of it being dreary and oppressive.

On the other hand, many scholarly historians refrain from using the label "Dark Ages" because of its misleading connotations. Europeans of the time did not see themselves in any type of Dark Ages, but scholars in the eighteenth and nineteenth centuries looked back on that period very critically. Thinking of themselves as advanced and the product of the Scientific Revolution, they labeled the period out of which society had emerged as dark. They labeled their own period as the Enlightenment referring to how they had embraced the light which freed them from the bondages of religion, tradition and ignorance.

The Dark Ages were difficult but not as dark, primitive or unscientific as many modern people think. Throughout the Middle Ages there was much progress made in technology and science. Historian Rodney Stark, in his excellent book entitled, *The Victory of Reason,* explains how watermills were developed and built across Europe. This provided for them what our modern motor does for us; people were enabled to efficiently cut lumber and stones, turn lathes, grind knives and swords, mechanize cloth making, hammer metal and make pulp to produce paper. Windmills were also employed to pump water for irrigation and the drainage of large wetlands.

Tremendous changes also happened throughout society as a result of the invention of glasses, chimneys and clocks. Versatile plows opened up huge areas for farming. The development of round ships and compasses opened up the world to travel by water. Land transportation was revolutionized by the invention of horse collars and wagons with brakes and front axles that could swivel.

Each of these changes were significant advancements but let's simply consider the invention of the chimney. Before homes had chimneys, people lived in unheated shelters or in homes filled with smoke. Without chimneys people smelled like smoke, breathed toxic air and often ate uncooked food. With chimneys as only one of many advancements we can be assured that life for the common people in the Middle Ages was better than it was for them during the Greek and Roman Empires.

The point is that civilization did not go backwards nor even stop advancing during the Middle Ages. An accurate view of Western civilization would see humanity constantly advancing technologically and scientifically.

38. Medieval Christianity

It was during the Middle Ages when Christianity spread across Europe and dramatically influenced its values. This is the very thing of which some historians are critical. Indeed, there were some negative outcomes that came with the expansion of Christianity which we will mention below, but on the positive side we can note that the Church and government more than any other factors displaced pagan views and established civilization.

For example, the murderous entertainment in the Roman Colosseum was quickly stopped by the advancing Church. The Colosseum went through many transitions at various times providing space for housing, workshops, churches and a religious order. Much of the tumbled stone was removed and then reused to build palaces, churches, hospitals and other buildings elsewhere in Rome. Pope Sixtus tried, but failed, to turn the building into a wool factory to provide employment for Rome's prostitutes. Such transformations were emblematic of the times, revealing the impact of Christian values. Those values came to permeate European society and they became enforced by civil law.

On the negative side we can agree with the more critical historians that the Church became oppressive and propagated superstitions. However, these errors should not be thought of as the exclusive fault of Church leaders. They were primarily the result of Christian thought making inroads into what remained of the oppressive Greek and Roman people, along with the barbarians who had previously inhabited the region. Uncivilized people still worshipped many gods and their lives were already filled with superstitions. The Greek and Roman fatalistic ideas held sway and people continued to believe that their lot in life was inescapable. Business and commerce were already looked down upon. Christianity did not bring these ideas but it did unfortunately incorporate many of these already existing beliefs.

The Church made further errors which negatively affected people in the Middle Ages. In particular, Church theologians like Augustine (354-430) over-emphasized the wickedness of humanity, which further caused people to think of themselves as victims. They saw themselves as so helplessly under the influence of sin that their only hope was to have something outside of themselves—namely the Church and government—rule over them. This furthered the oppression of the period.

Medieval Christianity was fatalistic. People accepted their lot in life and Church leaders taught that any person who wanted to get ahead was succumbing to the evil temptations of greed, avarice and pride. These values and beliefs had a profound impact upon economics of Europe during the Middle Ages.

39. A Morphed Form of Christianity

Medieval Christianity was very different than first century Christianity. The earlier form was strongly tied to its Jewish roots—roots which never emphasized the fatalism of the Greek and Romans, the wickedness of humanity, the need to have someone rule over them, the evils of doing business, nor the superstitions of the uncivilized world. In fact, ancient Jewish thought was so dominated by the concept of one God, that ideas of demons and angels were not very developed.[7] Furthermore, the Jews were fully given to the effectiveness of doing business and the resulting benefits of individual and corporate wealth, authority and abundance. With its Jewish foundation, Christianity of the first century was reassuring of the dignity of man and solidly grounded in a concept of God's people being the head in all areas of life.

When Christianity merged into the Greek and Roman worlds, it lost touch with its Jewish bearings. Plus there were a host of European people groups who held to myths and superstitions which influenced the Church. The outcome was a form of Christianity so different from first century Christianity that we can say Medieval Christianity was a morphed form of Christianity—a form of Christianity with which most modern Christians do not want to be associated.

40. Serfdom to Capitalism

The majority of Europeans during the early Middle Ages lived as serfs on land owned by kings or lords who ruled from fortified castles. They were trapped in subsistence living, but this was accepted because people had no concept of advancing from one class to a higher class. This worldview was supported by the teachings of the Medieval Church.

It is difficult for modern people to understand how profoundly the Church influenced the thoughts of the masses.

---

7 Only after 586 BC when the Southern tribes were taken into exile into Babylon did the Jews come under the influence of Babylonian thought and develop their understanding of spiritual beings opposing the will of God.

Some leaders challenged the teachings of the Church but it was difficult to get the masses to change without the Church's blessings. So the people changed but only as the Church changed and changes within economic spheres did not significantly come until the eleventh through twelfth centuries.

In the late Middle Ages Church monasteries played a major role in setting a new standard for work. In particular, the Benedictine monks lived by the Benedictine rule which demanded that brothers live by the labor of their own hands. This set a standard by which all Christians were to earn their own way. This lesson became even more pronounced when contrasted with the lifestyle of the Franciscan monks who taught that only by embracing poverty can the individual truly imitate Christ. In 1323, Pope John XXII condemned that Franciscan teaching as heretical. Today we can honor Francis of Assisi for his sacrificial living, for God may choose some individuals to live such a lifestyle, but the vast majority of humanity are created by God to work six days each week and support themselves.

During the twelfth and thirteenth centuries great thinkers such as Thomas Aquinas (A.D. 1225-1274) and other Catholic theologians strongly defended rights for personal property and personal gain.[8] It was during that period that we can see the Church reaching into its historical Jewish roots and returning to some economic values set forth in the Old Testament.

It was also during that period when many serfs left the farms and migrated to the towns and cities. This developed the need for merchants who could arrange for food and other supplies to be brought from the country into the populated areas. Money became a more common currency of exchange enabling more people to accumulate wealth. Then the plague

---

8 As early at the fifth century Augustine wrote about key issues related to buying and selling products.

(1348-1354) killed about one third of the population of Europe, decimating the labor force and allowing surviving serfs to take jobs which paid wages. Soon masses of laborers were able to enter into a labor force which ran more according to capitalistic principles.

41. Introduction of Business Standards and Ethics

During the eleventh through fourteenth centuries business accelerated and numerous guilds were formed to organize the various trades into associations. In the eleventh and twelfth centuries those guilds established guidelines for business. Then in the twelfth through fourteenth centuries there emerged Livery Companies which were solidly tied to the Church and dedicated to promote righteous ethics in business. At a time when dishonest scales and shady business practices were commonplace, the Livery Companies verified weights and measures, along with promoting high standards of excellence. By the fifteenth century the Livery Companies became so influential that they brought about a revolution in the business climate of Europe.[9]

Although some historians who are antagonistic toward Judaism and/or Christianity like to downplay this fact, capitalism was one of the major triumphs of the Judeo-Christian ethic over Greek and Roman thought. Capitalism was the system which freed the Western world from the greater oppression of the powerful over the mass of humanity by giving every person the opportunity to advance. Capitalism allowed a middle class to arise and displace the ruling aristocracy. It also catapulted the Western world ahead of other civilizations. (We will see this after the following discussion on Christian compassion.)

---

9 This discussion of Livery Companies taken from and is further developed in: Ken Elred. *God Is at Work* (Ventura, CA: Regal, 2005), p. 91-93.

42. Taking Care of the Widow, Orphan and Poor

Another triumph of Judeo-Christian values was the instilling of compassion in Western civilization.[10] As mentioned earlier, the ancient pagan religions offered no motives for charity. Stoic philosophers taught that it was disrespectful to associate with the weak or poor. Romans were callous and compassionless toward the needy. In contrast, the early Christians held to the Jewish value that all people are created in the image of God. As we discussed, Hebrew society had many ways of making provisions for the needy, including the giving of alms and farmers gleaning their crops only once so that the poor could freely gather that which was left behind.

From the very start, Christians cared for widows, orphans and the poor. Not only did they have this from their Hebrew roots, but also from the standard raised by Jesus whose very life was directed toward reaching out and loving others, especially the downtrodden. We can read in the book of Acts how the early disciples took care of the needy. Deacons were assigned for feeding widows (Acts 6:1-6). Peter and Paul were committed to caring for the poor (Gal. 2:10). The Church father, Tertullian, wrote how the Christians voluntarily contributed to a common fund for helping the poor.[11] Justin Martyr (ca. 100-166) wrote how collections were taken during church services to help orphans. There are many such references in the Christian writings of the period.

Throughout the last 2,000 years of Western history the Church has been at the forefront of building hospitals and running orphanages. During the thirteenth century a group known as the Order of the Holy Ghost operated more than 800 orphanages, and many monasteries cared for orphans

---

10 This discussion of Christian compassion was inspired by and is further developed in: Alvin Schmidt. *How Christianity Changed the World* (Grand Rapids, MI: Zondervan, 2004), p. 125-148.

11 *Apology* 39.

throughout the Middle Ages. Even today most Christian denominations collect funds to give clothing, food and medical relief to the poor.

The Judeo-Christian ethic was one of benevolent capitalism. People worked hard, lived frugally, saved and gave.

43. The Scientific Revolution

During the sixteenth century a revolution in thought took place that set Europe and eventually the whole Western world on a new accelerated path.

Previous to that revolution, people had a victimizational mind-set as a result of the Greek and Roman fatalism. This was worsened by the Medieval mind which thought of humanity as helplessly wicked and the world as controlled by spiritual beings including demons, angels and God.

One positive step out of victimizational living resulted from the writings of Thomas Aquinas (A.D. 1225-1274), who taught that man's will is fallen but not his intellect. This led to the understanding that man's intellect can arrive at truth, which opened the door for intellectual endeavors of all sorts, including the Scientific Revolution of the sixteenth and seventeenth centuries.

In that revolution, leaders set aside the myths and superstitions which had led people to believe that the world was tossed to and fro by spiritual beings. Leaders like Copernicus, Galileo, Newton and Bacon pioneered new areas of thought resulting in a belief that this world is governed by natural laws, and hence, it can be understood by people who will observe and study it.

Historians who are antagonist toward Christianity tend to present the Scientific Revolution as in opposition to Christianity, but actually the leaders of the Revolution, such as Copernicus, Galileo, Newton and Bacon, were all trained by the Church and they were strong theists. Furthermore, almost all scientific research of the period was financed by the Church. The most intense and well-know battle surrounded Galileo, but it was not a case of the Church against Galileo as some historians would have us believe. Many Church leaders, and especially the Jesuit priests, were on the side of Galileo. It was the scholars in universities who were primarily against him. It is most accurate to think of the battles of the Scientific Revolution as *internal battles*—that is, among Church leaders. In introducing their new ways of thinking, some God-fearing scientists had conflicts with certain Church leaders, but those conflicts were primarily the result of Medieval superstitions, not Judeo-Christian thought.[12] In fact, the very foundation of all scientific endeavors was the belief that there is one God and this world functions according to His laws.[13]

The Scientific Revolution impacted all areas of human life including economics because it transformed people from the victimizational mind-set into one of understanding and exercising authority over one's life and circumstances.

44. The Protestant Reformation

During the same period as the Scientific Revolution, came the Protestant Reformation which caused capitalism to take on greater fervency. Many scholars lay much of the credit (or blame, depending upon their perspective) at the feet of John Calvin. To his credit Calvin taught that all vocations are holy (as did Martin Luther); whether a person is a priest

---

12 For another example, consider how Copernicus's idea that the earth revolved around the sun was opposed by certain Church leaders, but the contrary view of the sun revolving around the earth was planted in Western thought primarily through Plato, not Hebrew or early Christian thought.

13 For further discussion on how the Scientific Revolution was founded on Christian thought and more particularly on monotheism see my book entitled: *Christianity Unshackled*.

or a merchant or a mason, God is equally pleased as long as each individual is fulfilling his or her calling. This freed the people from thinking that they must join a religious order if they really want to please God. It also lifted the stature of the common person to a level which would have seemed ridiculous to the ancient Greek and Roman minds. Later on, the Puritans carried this idea even further, emphasizing the importance of fulfilling one's God-given calling or vocation.

Calvin and other Protestant leaders also encouraged the aggressive pursuit of wealth through honest, hard work. Many historians have repeated the observation of the influential philosopher, Max Weber, who said that the spirit of capitalism was the unexpected by-product of the Protestant Reformation.

45. Attitudes towards Charging Interest

Attitudes toward lending money and charging interest also changed.

During the Middle Ages the Roman Catholic Church taught that charging interest was sinful, and referred to it as usury. In the Lateran Council of 1139, they went so far as to pronounce and publish a severe judgment against all usurers.

The Jews of the period had a very different view of charging interest. In fact, Jewish businessmen had dominated the lending services during the Middle Ages even though they were despised for doing so. As explained earlier, they believed that lending money at interest was evidence of God's blessing on their lives. They would not lend with interest to other Jews, but they were happy to lend to Christians.

Where did the Church get its negative view of charging interest? First and foremost, from the Greek and Roman worldview. Business and commerce were already looked down upon, but then philosophers like Aristotle taught that charging interest is unnatural, and therefore, unjust. Church leaders reinforced this view by quoting the Hebrews Scriptures which give instructions not to charge interest when lending money to one's brothers. The Church extended the reference to "brothers" beyond familial relationships and said that all Christians are brothers and sisters. With that understanding, the related Scriptures were interpreted to mean that usury is always wrong. But it is doubtful that the Church would have applied these Scriptures with such a firm hand if it had not been so strongly influenced by Aristotle. If Christians had a more positive view of business and commerce they would have thought more like the Jews that charging interest—at least of outsiders—is a blessing from God.

It was John Calvin and other leaders of the Protestant Reformation who taught that charging interest is justified for the purpose of commerce. The Protestant reformers never would have approved of some of our modern use of credit, such as what we see in the use of credit cards. However, they would have agreed that if a person is going to make a profit using someone else's money, then the lender should share in that profit by charging interest.

46. European Commercialization

During the late sixteenth century the Dutch-speaking citizens of the Netherlands were the most commerce-oriented people of Europe and they dominated world commerce for several reasons. First, they embraced Calvinism with its strong emphasis on doing business and working hard. The Netherlands was also a haven for Jews who excelled in business. And third, the Dutch were foremost as seagoing merchants, eventually starting investment companies to finance their worldwide shipping industry.

England did not lag far behind while the rest of Europe watched and then followed. With robust capitalism came abundance. Modern historians sometimes refer to the period as the Age of Commercialization. This label came from the fact that people began to produce products for others, that is, commercially, rather than just what their own family could consume or use. Those products were sold so individuals could make a profit and accumulate wealth. As this commercialization advanced, people were able to specialize in the production of one product, and hence, produce increased quantities.

This societal transformation went hand-in-hand with an agricultural revolution. Before the premodern period, about 80 percent of the entire population was required to work in agriculture just to produce enough food for all of the people. Even with that great workforce, famines regularly followed unfavorable weather conditions. Better tools and new farming practices gradually transformed agricultural practices so that by 1900 less than 10 percent of the population was needed to produce all of the necessary food. This released a work force to serve in other areas. At the same time an abundance of food eliminated the fear of future famines, resulting in a new sense of security so people were more willing to invest their accumulated wealth in new products and business ventures.[14]

47. European Expansion through Colonization

As mentioned earlier, capitalism catapulted the Western world ahead of other civilizations. This is evident in the fact that the countries of Europe were soon able to colonize regions across the globe. Britain, France, Spain, Portugal and

---

14 For a more thorough discussion of this agricultural revolution see: Joyce Appleby. *A History of Capitalism* (New York, NY: W. W. Norton & Company, Inc., 2010), p. 56-86.

the Netherlands claimed territories in Africa, Asia, Australia, North American and South America. Europeans took dominion over more than 50 percent of the earth. The same principles which allowed the Jews to prosper allowed Europe to rise to the top, or as God's promise said, to be the head and not the tail.

Of course, colonization led to many abusive situations with conquering people exploiting the labor and resources of the subjugated ones. Individual capitalists seized the opportunities to make profits by taking and then importing gold, silver, diamonds, ivory, spices, silk, tobacco, rubber, foods and slaves. When countries got involved, the takeovers became especially brutal and native people suffered greatly. Some crops such as sugar could only be grown in certain climates and soils, so European countries fought for control of those lands.

As mentioned earlier, capitalism without godly values can be destructive. It can lead to the rich oppressing the poor, which it definitely did in the seventeenth through twentieth centuries.

On the more positive side, Christianity spread as European nations colonized much of the world. Missionary activity became especially active during the nineteenth century. In 1750, 22 percent of the world called itself Christian. By 1900, 34 percent of the world called itself Christian.[15] Of course, this is no justification for the abuse and oppression resulting from colonization, but it is a historical fact that the spread of Christianity moved hand-in-hand with expanding business.

48. Redefining Self-interest As Good

For capitalism to be fully released, there had to be a fundamental change in how Europeans understood human nature.

---

15 Ken Eldred. *God Is at Work* (Ventura, CA: Regal Books, 2005), p.43.

Ever since the time of Augustine, the Church had emphasized the wickedness and corruption of humanity. This is a central reason why people during the Middle Ages saw the pursuit of wealth or any pursuit involving self-interest as evil.

One of many philosophers who challenged this view was Thomas Hobbs (1588-1679) who wrote a book entitled, *Leviathan*, in which he contended that the pursuit of personal well-being is good. Voltaire (1694-1778) further developed this view and taught that every individual should pursue their own wealth. Other thinkers such as Rousseau and Locke tried to develop a government corresponding to a freer and more positive view of human nature.

These thinkers had opposition coming from the Church, however, it is worth mentioning again that the Church was under the influence of Augustine and other leaders with similar teachings. If the Church had held to its Jewish roots it would have always held a more positive view of human nature and it would have recognized the more positive aspects of the personal pursuit of wealth.

49. Free Market Capitalism

With a more positive view of human nature, many philosophers concluded that the path to a healthy society is to allow every person to purse their own happiness. During the seventeenth and eighteenth centuries, French economists applied this to economics, and hence, urged governments to stop interfering in foreign trade. This idea was referred to as *laissez faire,* which developed into the idea that trade, business and industry should operate with as little as possible control from the government.

During the same period Adam Smith wrote *Wealth of Nations,* in which he encouraged "free enterprise," the idea that the forces of supply and demand will best control the markets.[16, 17] Incorporating these ideas resulted in a more aggressive form of capitalism, and in fact, many economists will only call laissez faire capitalism or free market capitalism true capitalism.

For our discussion it will be important to know that laissez faire capitalism had as a foundation the belief that people are good and the pursuit of personal wealth is good. Personally, I believe that some personal pursuit is good and some is bad; therefore I cannot fully embrace laissez faire capitalism. I believe in capitalism, but later I will explain how it must be governed wisely.

50. Freedom and Capitalism in America

The United States was founded in the intellectual and social climate of the eighteenth century. The opportunity to implement those beliefs came when the early colonists became fed up with the British rules which interfered with the normal production of goods and services.[18] The influence of French thinkers can be seen in the Declaration of Independence which states a belief in the dignity and freedom of humanity:

> We hold these truths to be self-evident, that all men are created equal, that they are endowed by their Creator with certain unalienable Rights, that among these are Life, Liberty and the pursuit of Happiness.

Note that the U.S. founding fathers had embraced the idea

---

16 Some historians consider Adam Smith the father of modern capitalism.

17 Although Adam Smith saw self-interest as the driving force of a healthy economy, he did not agree with Thomas Hobbs that all self-interest is good.

18 Just as important was the idea of taxation without representation.

that every person should be free to pursue their own personal happiness, and this they believed was good.

It is also worth noting that for the first time in human history a nation recognized that sovereignty rested with the individual rather than with a king, emperor or a few elites ruling from the top.

This was a radical change and positive step. However, it would be a mistake to equate the American concept of individual freedom with the ancient Hebrew understanding. Freedom for a Hebrew meant that a person was free from slavery, domination or oppression of a foreign nation. However, it did not refer to freedom in the sense of total independence. Ideally, the Hebrews saw themselves as free to serve God and bring their lives into alignment with His Laws. Individual sovereignty in the sense of governing oneself would have been thought of as anarchy. In spite of this discrepancy between the American understanding and the ancient Hebrew understanding, the *Declaration of Independence* was a historic step in the right direction of individual freedom.

51. The Fruit of Capitalism

The most significant demonstration of what free people can do in a capitalistic society has been the United States. By 1903, America became the richest country in the world.[19] Today with less than five percent of the world's population, America owns 32.6 percent of the world's wealth[20] and, with six percent of the world's land area, produces almost 25 percent of the world's food.[21] Individual freedom and free

---

19 Stephen Moore and Julian Simon. *It's Getting Better All the Time* (Washington, D.C.: Cato Institute, 2000), p.60.

20 From a report in 2000, cited in: www.nytimes.com/2006/-12/06/business/worldbusiness/06wealth.html

21 Stephen Moore and Julian Simon. *It's Getting Better All the Time* (Washington, D.C.: Cato Institute, 2000), p. 94.

enterprise have cultivated risk taking, innovation, scientific exploration and societal advancement on a grand scale that has never occurred anywhere before. This is evidence of what the human spirit—which is created in the image of God—can produce when unfettered by oppressive government.

52. The Industrial Revolution

Recognizing the incredible potential which capitalism is able to release, we must also consider the abuses and flaws. These were very evident during the colonization period and also during the Industrial Revolution which began in England in the late 1700's, then moved into North America in the 1800's, and finally across all of Europe. Manufacturing was taken out of the homes and workshops, and brought into the factories in the cities. This was facilitated by innovations making use of steam and electricity. Masses of people migrated from rural to urban areas. While the industrialization of society improved the quality of life for most people, the average laborer worked under horrible conditions. Sanitation was poor, work hours long and pay low. The laborers had little to no rights.

53. Karl Marx's Solution

With hopes of bringing relief to the working class, Karl Marx (1818-1883) developed the foundation for communism, the economic and political system which places ownership of all property in the hands of the state, along with control of production, labor and distribution. Communism differs from socialism in that communism calls for armed force or outside intervention to impose its goals on society. In contrast, advocates of socialism seek to promote similar goals, but primarily through education, election and legislation. Communism is also more encompassing, seeking to control social and cultural life based in atheism.

Seeing the relationship between Judaism and capitalism Karl Marx made plain his anti-Semitic beliefs in his book entitled, *On the Jewish Question.* Throughout his life Marx endeavored to overthrow capitalism and any economic ideas associated with Judaism and Christianity. He boldly predicted the overthrow of capitalism, but at the present time capitalism is a shining light above communism.

54. Governing Capitalism Wisely

It was not only Karl Marx who saw the flaws of laissez faire capitalism. Almost everyone was aware of the plight of the working class during the industrial revolution. In some of the worst situations the capitalists who owned factories or mines would provide housing and food for the workers whom they employed. After deducting rent and food costs, the employees would end up owing more money to their boss than they had earned after working 70 or more hours during the week. Anyone can see that such treatment was wrong.

The rights of workers needed to be protected. The abuses evident during the Industrial Revolution taught us that capitalism needs to be regulated. So too, the abuses evident during the colonization period made it clear that unregulated capitalism can lead to oppression of the masses and depletion of natural resources.

If individuals would conduct their lives according to godly values, we would not need to regulate capitalism. Unfortunately, people can be abusive. In their personal pursuit of happiness they can harm others. For this reason laws must be made and enforced. As the apostle Paul wrote:

[The] *law is not made for a righteous person, but*

*for those who are lawless and rebellious, for the
ungodly and sinners...*

(I Tim. 1:9)

Capitalism is good, but we must keep the system in check
because of human sinfulness.

55. Capitalism Tempered with Socialistic Values

Laws which govern capitalism are (hopefully) stirred by
social concerns, that is, concerns for the welfare of individuals. Therefore, restrictions on capitalism typically move us in
the direction of socialism.

To show this relationship I will place capitalism and socialism at two different ends of a spectrum. As explained,
laissez faire capitalism is the economic system governed only
by free markets, with little to no government control. The
more we move in the direction of socialism the more we see
government regulations and controls on the economy.

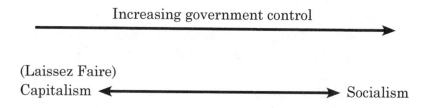

Increasing government control

(Laissez Faire)
Capitalism ← → Socialism

From this point forward I will refer to advocates of laissez
faire capitalism as "purist capitalists." They are the ones who
long to a return to little or no government restrictions.

56. Moves Towards Socialistic Values

Let's consider a few of the socialistic moves made in the U.S. during the last 200 years.

In the middle of the nineteenth century, several Anglican clergymen led a movement to bring reform by promoting trade unions, adult education and social insurance for workers. Sooner or later, these actions would have been taken without the help and encouragement of the Church, but at the time, common people were greatly influenced by religious leaders, and hence, the Church's endorsement was key.

During the same period, the Roman Catholic Church acted to limit economic injustices. Most notably, Pope Leo XIII had his *Rerum Novarum* published (1891) in which he urged labor reform, a minimum wage, a limit on hours of work and restrictions on child labor. Later the Roman Church organized a group called *Catholic Action,* which became very active in the labor movement.

In the early 1900's, many church leaders took up the cause of the oppressed in a movement coined the *Social Gospel.* They attempted to further the kingdom of God by bringing in more just and fair laws.

In the United States, President Woodrow Wilson was an early champion of the Social Gospel and he succeeded in ensuring an eight-hour work day for railroad workers and establishing national standards for protecting child labor. He also backed restrictions on corporate trusts and created the Federal Reserve to ensure the stability of banking.

Both positives and negatives developed out of each of these socialistic moves. Purist capitalists denounce those changes and call for a return to laissez faire or free market capitalism. Modern socialists call for even more government regulation.

57. The New Deal in the America

The greatest moves in the twentieth century toward social reform came under President Franklin D. Roosevelt. His administration, with the support of congress, established the *New Deal*. This included a series of decisions in the 1930's such as *The Social Security Act* which provided pensions for the aged, insurance for the unemployed and payments for needy children, the blind and the disabled. *The National Labor Relations Act* guaranteed workers the right to organize unions. *The Securities and Exchange Commission* was formed to regulate the sale of securities and to hinder unfair stock market practices. *The National Recovery Administration* was created to enforce codes of fair business and industry practices. *The Fair Labor Standards Act* set a minimum wage and maximum workweek of 44 hours; it also banned children under 16 years of age from working in factories and during school hours. President Roosevelt acted during the "Dust Bowl" years of the 1930's which devastated much of the farmland in the Midwest; his actions provided for and allowed millions of American farmers to keep their farms in the midst of the worst draught in U.S. history.

Ever since Roosevelt's New Deal, the United States government has taken a more active role in governing the economic growth of the nation and ensuring the economic security of the people (although purist capitalists consider almost all of it government interference).

58. Modern Capitalism Versus Socialism

Today in the U.S. we have a capitalistic economy but it has been tempered with socialistic values. Although purist capitalists bemoan every new move toward socialism, few Americans would choose to go back to the pre-twentieth century economy which allowed for great abuses of the common laborer and turned a blind eye to the needs of the elderly, children and infirm.

Since the mid-1800s, most Western countries have taken actions to ensure the rights of laborers and force more equitable distribution of their nation's wealth. As a result of restrictions on capitalism and increasing social programs, most Western countries have moved in the direction of socialism. Most European countries are even more socialistic than the U.S. with many state-owned or state subsidized industries and services.

59. Economists Shaping Society

During the twentieth century two economists stand out as leaders who have shaped thought and policies. John Mainard Keynes was the economist who worked alongside of President Roosevelt and encouraged deficit spending—that the government should spend more than it is bringing in for the purpose of stimulating the economy. At the other end of the spectrum was Milton Friedman, who received the Nobel Prize for his work which challenged the ideas of Keynes. Friedman is considered by many to be the father of modern capitalism.

60. Environmental Protection

Finally it is important to note how environmental concerns have played a significant role in economic development.

During the Industrial Revolution, unrestrained capitalism showed little to no regard for the environment. With factories operating at full speed, heavily populated areas became cesspools of filth. Black clouds settled over major cities and soot blanketed the buildings and streets. With little to no government regulation, rivers were polluted and lands were raped of their resources.

We can see the obvious abuses as we look back upon that period, but we would develop a distorted understanding if we only judged the period with our modern value system. It has been in recent years that people have become acutely aware of the need to protect our environment. Even if the common people of the nineteenth century had the authority to impose restrictions on factories they probably would not have done so. America was thought of as an endless land with thousands of unexplored regions. Resources were seen as unlimited. The earth was considered God's gift for humanity's use. As a result, even if the government had been able to control business, little thought would have been given to the need for environmental protection.

It is from our modern perspective that we can see the need to protect our environment and resources. Every year more laws are enacted toward this goal. Those laws and restrictions are often burdensome upon those launching capitalistic ventures. Environmental studies may be required which take great investments and years to complete. Increasingly restrictive standards cost companies huge amounts of money and can result in financial collapse. Society continues to struggle for a balance between protection of our environment and freedom for individuals and business.

Summary

To summarize this section we can say that capitalism is part of the Judeo-Christian ethic. In saying this, it is important to note that both aspects—Judeo and Christian—are essential. Historians who are antagonistic toward Christianity tend to isolate Christianity from Judaism and then equate historic Christianity with the Church of the Middle Ages. The Middle Ages were difficult times and most modern Christians are not proud of the version of Christianity evident during that period. Concerning economics, the established Church was oppressive, over-emphasized the wickedness of humanity, supported the serf system, condemned the charging of interest and was down on business and commerce. None of those values reflect the values held by ancient Hebrew society.

It is most accurate to think of the Middle Ages, not as the period in which Christianity was dominant, but as the period in which Christian thought was just beginning to make inroads into what remained of the oppressive Greek and Roman empires.

When Judeo-Christian ethics finally rose to prominence during the late Middle Ages, it was Church leaders who taught the importance of property ownership and the rights for personal advancement. Christian leaders began asserting ethics into the business world. It was also the Church which promoted compassion and established many programs which cared for orphans, widows and other needy individuals.

During the sixteenth century the Scientific Revolution broke people free of the victimizational mind-set resulting from a worldview which saw demons, angels and God tossing the world to and fro. Once the Judeo understanding that there is only one God became fixed in the minds of leaders, they deduced that this world runs according to His laws; then they set out to understand this world. They also took the reigns to manage this world when they embraced a world-view much like that of the Jewish people who understood that God placed us here to take dominion of this world and manage it well.

With the Protestant Reformation of the sixteen and seventeen century, capitalism took on greater fervency. Christians were taught to be industrious. The condemnation of charging interest was lifted. Businesspeople rose to the new world of opportunities. These changes, along with other capitalistic values, allowed Europe to rise to the top and colonize most of the world.

During the eighteenth and nineteenth centuries, European people began embracing a sense of the dignity of humanity. Philosophers of the period impacted all of society and people began to think of their efforts to improve their own lot in life as good.

Finally, capitalism came to dominate the business world during the Industrial Revolution. But when abuses became evident, it was primarily Church leaders and then political leaders with the support of the Church, who rose up with social concerns and promoted legal action which supported the rights of laborers.

Some historians downplay the significance of the Judeo-Christian ethic in the development of capitalism. They often depict capitalism as not even forming until the sixteenth to eighteenth centuries. It is true that serious discussions of economics and even the word capitalism was not in use until the eighteenth century, but all of the foundations of compassionate capitalism were laid down in ancient Hebrew society. They disappeared for a time while Christianity was emerging into the European barbarism of the Middle Ages, but the Judeo-Christian ethics re-surfaced and took prominence during the Modern Period.

In conclusion of this section, we can say that capitalism is good. It creates an economic environment in which the human spirit is free to dream, initiate and act. However, there are flaws in laissez faire capitalism. If people are not governed, they can and sometimes have taken advantage of the less fortunate. Unscrupulous capitalists have also depleted our resources and wreaked havoc on our environment. The answer is not to get rid of capitalism, as Karl Marx attempted to do, but rather to keep our foundation of a capitalistic economy while governing wisely (and develop a culture of compassion, which we will discuss in Section V).

Section IV
Capitalism at Work Today

I am not an economist. As mentioned earlier, I am a Christian teacher who understands history and the development of Western thought. I have also traveled the world extensively and I am aware of the economic restraints on the common people in underdeveloped nations. Within my field of expertise, there are a few truths which are obvious.

Most importantly, we need the energy of the human spirit which only capitalism can release. However, we need to govern wisely. Let's apply these lessons to the modern world.

61. Capitalism at Work in Developing Nations

My experience in underdeveloped countries came as a result of helping dozens of churches get established in remote regions of the world. I have learned that people need more than a church. They need jobs, clean water, education, safety and health care. All of these things come hand-in-hand with business.

Of course, not everyone benefits from business development, especially in countries where corruption is rampant. When big oil companies or mining industries develop, outsiders come and take local resources while the political elite and the wealthy find ways to take the vast amount of wealth generated. Of course, locals who are employed by the big companies benefit, but the big industries often employ specialists from outside. In those situations the only nationals benefiting are the political leaders in power. This is no reason to stop development. Rather it is a reason to work for the elimination of corruption and the development of programs through which the local people can benefit.

When we talk about businesses on a smaller scale, local people benefit more directly. In deciding how much business to send them, the most important thing to know is that people in developing nations *want* businesses to come to their regions. For the most part, they *want capitalists* to come. They want the opportunities which only business can provide. Unless a person realizes this, they cannot make wise decisions as to how much of our capitalistic ventures should be allowed in the poorer regions of the world.

62. McDonald's Moving into an African Village

Consider a McDonald's restaurant being built in a poverty-stricken, remote village of Africa. Admittedly, this is probably not the business most needed by poor village people, however, I am taking an extreme example to make my point. Also, it is good to talk about McDonald's because it is the corporation (along with Walmart) which is most often criticized by socialists for employing people at low wages, and for serving high fat, less healthy food. McDonald's also seems to represent to socialists the commercial values of the Western capitalistic world.

Consider what changes will actually occur if McDonald's decides to build a restaurant in a remote, poverty-stricken African village. First, the McDonald's corporation representatives are going to determine how safe the region is, including limited thievery, police protection and assurance that no war will break out. Second, they will determine if the local government honors the rights for personal property ownership. If there is no assurance that their investment will be secure, they probably will not build. If they are determined to build anyway, they will put pressure on the government to establish security and safety, along with property rights.

These are great benefits which business brings to underdeveloped regions.

Next, the McDonald's representatives will determine how well supplies can be transported to the restaurant. In particular, there must be suitable roads. Also, there has to be dependable sources of clean water, sewage and electricity. If these are not available, it is very unlikely that any restaurant will be built. If McDonald's is determined to build anyway, they will put pressure on the government to build roads and provide the necessary water, sewage and electricity.

Even the possibility of building a restaurant in an undeveloped area catches and focuses the attention of the local and national governments. Previously overlooked areas are examined, populations are studied and potential for future development is determined. With government attention comes government support and financial aid.

Progress will be made in each of the following areas even before a McDonald's restaurant is built:

1) steps to limit thievery;
2) increased police protection;
3) reduced risk of war;
4) personal property rights ensured;
5) construction of suitable roads;
6) development of a clean water source;
7) provision of sewage and dependable utilities;
8) government support and financial aid.

None of these things are likely to develop if McDonald's or some other influential business is unwilling to venture into that village. Government lives off of taxes and eagerly makes room for business. It will take a corporation of significant influence to put enough pressure on the government to make these changes.

63. McDonald's Benefitting the African Village

As the McDonald's restaurant is being constructed, the local economy will receive more money than at any time in its history. When the restaurant opens for business, new employees will be trained and paid a salary. Almost all of the income they make will end up in their own community because those employees will buy local goods and provide for their families. The restaurant will also buy locally what is available, such as potatoes and corn, further helping the economy.[22]

Of course, McDonald's is only going to carry on with its business if it can take more money out than it puts in. But very little of that money will come out of the pockets of the poor. The majority of local people will be too poor to buy a meal from the restaurant. Those who do will probably spend a day's wages to buy the cheapest hamburger on some special day such as their child's birthday. The majority of business will come from the few wealthy residents and tourists passing through the area. Their money will flow through the restaurant with a significant portion flowing through the hands of the employees and, hence, into the local economy.

Once the McDonald's restaurant is in business, an entire business district will develop as native people choose to locate their own businesses as close as possible to the restaurant. They will do this because there is already a paved road, electricity, clean water, a stream of customers and police protection. Tourists who previously drove through the village without stopping will be happy to see the golden arches and merchants selling locally-made products. The tourism industry will increase because such locations become shopping centers for people traveling through the region.

---

22 McDonald's attempts to offer some local products. For example I have eaten rice with my Big Mac in the Philippines and I have seen beer served at a McDonald's in Germany.

Although it is difficult for the modern technologically-advanced Western person to understand, the restaurant will become a symbol of pride, proof to the masses that the local natives are no longer excluded from the rest of the modern world. Hope will rise in the hearts of the people. Parents will be more motivated to encourage their children to get an education with expectations of escaping generational poverty. Believe it or not, the golden arches symbolize hope for the future.

For these reasons I wish more McDonald's restaurants would open up in the villages I work with in Africa. Of course, there are other businesses that may accomplish similar or even greater things, but I want whatever help we can get for the people I love in the poverty-stricken regions of the world.

64. Critics of McDonald's

Critics of capitalism could observe McDonald's moving into the local African village and raise their objections. They will most likely complain that the employees will be making low wages and the quality of food is not up to the highest standards.

Concerning the wages, people in developed nations need to be more aware of the critical conditions in poverty-stricken areas. In many regions in which I travel, the unemployment rate is over 80 percent. The reason people take jobs which seem to us as low-paying is because those are the best paying jobs in the region. Certainly we can encourage and even put pressure on corporations to pay better wages to their people, but make no mistake that in most cases corporations which are active in poorer areas are already paying the highest wages in that region.

It is also worth discussing the quality of food since modern

Westerners often ridicule the fast-food industry. This issue can only be addressed if we know the already-existing conditions of the local people. The people I eat with in many of those villages regularly experience famine, usually they have parasites throughout their bodies and they often have worms crawling out of their anus. The native foods tend to be fresher, however, a free-ranging chicken is typically ranging through garbage and sewage. It is no surprise that the life expectancy of people in such areas can be as low as 35 years. The truth is that McDonald's food is much cleaner and more nutritious than the natural, native foods. This is difficult for outsiders to understand, but it is a fact that people need to face before they try to stop a McDonald's from being built in an impoverished area.

65. Capitalism at Work in Africa

For another example of capitalism at work, let me tell you about a region of Africa where the people experience two seasons: a wet season and a dry season. Because of this they have a growing season followed by a season when food is often scarce. One of the main foods is potatoes. Each rainy season the farmers only grow what can be eaten within six months because they have no way to store potatoes; any potatoes older than six months will rot or be eaten by vermin. As a consequence, the people in remote regions go through different levels of famine during each dry season. Even now as I write these words, I have friends in Northern Kenya who are hungry and cannot feed their children. It is usually the children and elderly who die in such conditions. For them, poverty is a prison, with everyone living in mud huts, little to no medical services and schools with dirt floors and few books.

Into this picture, let's insert one capitalist with some capital. This capitalist erects a storage facility where potatoes can be cooled and kept for future use. During the growing season the capitalist buys from the area farmers as many potatoes as they can produce. Potatoes in the wet season are worth half as much as they are during the dry season. So the capitalist takes advantage of this difference and sells the potatoes back to the local people when the dry season comes.

The farmers can now grow more potatoes than before. In the past, they only grew as many as could be eaten before the potatoes would rot. Now they can sell their extra potatoes and make a profit, hence, changing their entire lifestyle. As time goes on, the owner of that potato warehouse may become successful enough to start shipping and selling potatoes to people living in the nearby cities and throughout the country. As a result, the farmers can sell as many potatoes as they can grow and the entire economy of the region will be transformed.

After the warehouse owner starts marketing potatoes outside of the region it would be to his benefit if water was made available throughout the region so that farmers can irrigate their crops to extend the growing season and increase the harvests. Perhaps the capitalist will someday be wealthy enough to build water reservoirs and irrigation systems, but it is more likely that he will use his influence to encourage the government to get involved.

Another transition will come as a result of the business owner influencing the government to provide a safe environment for ongoing business. No business owner is going to build a business where thieves and murderers are free to roam and act as they will. Governments know this and they will work hard at establishing order where they want to see businesses develop.

As the region becomes secure and begins to prosper, other capitalists will emerge. They will increase the economy and well-being of the local residents by bringing in more products to sell and by identifying local products which can be marketed outside of the region. Eventually they will also have enough influence to ensure the construction of schools, roads and hospitals. Along with this comes infrastructure including sewer systems, electricity, telephones and police enforcement to establish safety and order.

Each of these advancements are huge benefits, which people in developed nations take for granted. The development of a sewer system all by itself will dramatically improve the quality of life. Mosquitoes which carry malaria—the number one killer in many developing nations—will have fewer breeding grounds. The drinking water is less likely to be contaminated with sewage and the free-ranging chickens will stop eating exposed sewage. Not to mention the stench which people in poorer regions typically live in everyday.

Note the complete transformation: people were starving, helpless and living in huts with dirt floors; add capitalism and soon there will be work, food, education, safety, health care and hope for advancement.

66. A Critique from a Socialist

The illustration which I just offered of capitalism working in an underdeveloped nation can be analyzed through the eyes of a purist socialist and be seen quite differently. Instead of focusing on how the economy of the region is being transformed, we can focus on how the region is being pillaged of its natural resources and how the capitalist who owns the potato storage facility is getting rich off of the labor of the poor local farmers. Things seem so unfair. A socialist may try to correct things and his first course of action will be to create class warfare in which the poor farmers are stirred to take action against the rich capitalist. The socialist's end goal will be to get the government to come in and take the potato storage facility away from the capitalist and run it for the good of all.

Unfortunately, if the government takes over, success will be dramatically reduced. History is clear that government is not as good at running businesses as owners are. Owners are constantly motivated to increase in every area of business, including quality, efficiency, production, marketing, etc. In contrast, government-run businesses are administratively top-heavy and cumbersome, unable to adapt to changing conditions. Administrators and employees who have salaries and security established by the government have little reason to improve. Such a relationship set up between the employees and government tends to create a slave-like, you-take-care-of-me mind-set. Plus, the threat of the government taking over the potato business is going to keep other capitalists from coming into the area and investing. As a result, the local people will remain imprisoned in poverty for the rest of their lives.

Rather than imposing socialism, it would be to the benefit of all if the potato warehouse was left in the hands of the private owner. Of course, we need to govern wisely and we can incorporate some social values. For example, if a famine returns, the government may partner with the business owner to get potatoes back into the hands of the people. The government would also be wise to encourage other capitalists to come into the area and open up other businesses, including other potato warehouses which will offer competitive prices for the potatoes produced by the farmers. The workers must also be free to organize and negotiate for better prices and benefits. They may even want to develop some type of co-op in which the farmers can be part owners of a potato warehouse. Just as the capitalistic warehouse owner is free, so too the laborers must be free.

67. Do the Rich Get Richer and the Poor Poorer?

In a capitalistic society the rich usually do get richer, but the idea of the poor getting poorer is not typically the case (except where there is gross corruption). As we saw in the example of the capitalist's potato warehouse, all people benefited. Such transformation is the common experience rather than the exception to the rule.

It is in corrupt and non-capitalistic societies where businesses get poorer and the poor get poorer. We have seen this throughout history. In ancient civilizations such as the Assyrian, Egyptian, Persian, Greek and Roman, less than five percent of the populace enjoyed wealth, while over 90 percent were slaves or locked into subsistence living. Along with poverty came famines, diseases, thievery, murder and war. Similarly today in third-world countries, there are typically a few at the top who are extremely wealthy, while the masses live trapped in poverty, hoping to survive day-by-day.

Such disparity has also been evident during the last century in countries embracing socialism where their economic policies have wreaked havoc. Consider China's collectivist agricultural policies which choked initiative and left tens of millions starved to death—the worst mass starvation in recorded history. Or think of the thousands upon thousands of Russians who starved in the 1930's even though Russia has rich, fertile farmlands. Look also at the poverty of North Korea next to the thriving economy of South Korea. As Henry Grady Weaver wrote, *"Whenever a socialistic community is set up alongside of a community with a free economy, the contrast is too great to be ignored."*[23]

Capitalism is the economic system which God has given to humanity. It is the system which frees the human spirit

---

23 Henry Grady Weaver. *The Mainspring of Human Progress* (Hudson, NY: Foundation for Economic Education, 1953) p.49.

so that the masses can escape oppression, famines, plagues and war. Even more hope-creating is the fact that the poor almost always make dramatic economic advancements when capitalism is introduced to a society. The truth is that all people in capitalistic societies usually benefit. If those who want to excel financially are allowed to excel, the rich get richer and the poor get richer.

68. The Plight of the Poor

Of course, we all want to end poverty, but we can learn from history that capitalism—when governed wisely—is the most successful way to reach this goal. We need just laws and godly values with a capitalistic economy, but make no mistake that capitalism, not socialism, is the path to eliminate poverty.

Trying to disprove this fact, socialists will sometimes report that the percentage of poor people in the U.S. has been constantly increasing. But they can only say that by repeatedly elevating their standards by which they measure who is poor. What is considered the poverty level in the United States today is *three times more than the average income of the rest of the world.* To anyone who travels in underdeveloped countries it is obvious that the American standard of living is very high. In many regions where I have worked anyone who owns shoes is not considered poor. A common international poverty line is roughly $1 a day (or more precisely $1.25 a day).[24] Among poor people throughout the world a commonly shared standard is anyone who has a place to sleep and eats one meal a day is not poor.

In contrast, we can note the statistics of household under the poverty level in America: almost 70 percent own a car or truck, 98 percent own a refrigerator, and 95 percent own

24 http://en.wikipedia.org/wiki/Poverty_threshold

a television set. The average poor household in America is more likely to own a colored television set than the average income household in Ireland, France, Germany or Italy.[25] I do not want to minimize the suffering of those who are indeed locked in poverty, but America is a good place to be poor.

69. Socialism Is Cruel

Socialists tend to see capitalism as cruel because of the competition induced among the people and the fact that those who are less competitive experience less success. To eliminate competition and the resulting unfairness, purist socialists want to eliminate the upper class and evenly distribute all wealth.

To see this through different eyes, compare a capitalistic society to a rain forest where trees form a canopy high above the forest floor. The rainforest is the most diverse environment on earth, supporting more than two thirds of all the earth's plant and animal species. Even though rain forests cover less than six percent of the world's surface, 25 percent of all medicinal drugs are derived from ingredients produced there. Nowhere else on earth is there such a diversity and abundance.

Of course, there is competition and a struggle for every living thing to survive in the rainforest. Most obviously the tall trees hinder the amount of light which reaches the forest floor, hence limiting the growth of plants near the ground. A person who looks at the rainforest with a perspective analogous to a socialist's may conclude that we should cut down the tall trees so the forest floor can share in a greater portion of the light.

What will result? The forest floor will burst in growth and a jungle will form. Then the tree cutters may feel they have

25 Henry Grady Weaver. *The Mainspring of Human Progress*, p.76.

been successful in making all things fair. In reality, much of the diversity of life will disappear because the majority of animal species were living in the canopy, thriving on what the tall trees produced. Furthermore, cutting down the tall trees does not decrease competition, but only moves it to the forest floor.

Similarly under socialism, people are no less competitive. In fact, because food and supplies become more scare, competition becomes more covert, people fight to stand in lines to get needed resources, sales through black markets flourish and individuals hoard the things they can obtain. Under socialism people tend to become even more oriented toward every person for themselves.

Henry Grady Weaver said it well:

It may be argued, and it frequently is, that free competition is a ruthless and cruel process. But it is not nearly so ruthless and cruel as the opposite philosophy, which down through the ages has kept the majority of people ill-fed, ill-housed, ill-clothed, embroiled in wars, and dying of famine and pestilence.[26]

70. Capitalism Promotes Cooperation

Socialists miss how capitalists succeed primarily through cooperation, not competition. Consider again the rainforest. There is an endless number of symbiotic relationships with plants and animals totally dependent upon each other. The flower provides nectar for the bee, and the bee pollinates the flower. Such relationships are innumerable and every species depends on other species. Of course, there is competition within a species, but the most successful species are those

---

26 Henry Grady Weaver. *The Mainspring of Human Progress*, p. 240.

which adapt in order to cooperate with other species in the environment. Similarly, successful capitalists will compete with others who offer the same products, but they want prosperity for everyone else who offers different products. Capitalism works best when everyone helps each other and everyone prospers.

Anyone who is successful at capitalism understands this. It is the financially unsuccessful person who does not grasp this truth. In capitalism, prosperity for all is the key to prosperity for the individual. Diversity is the key to productivity. When a society encourages its people to pursue their dreams and rise to the maximum level of their productivity, differences emerge but the society in total benefits economically and culturally.

71. Relationships Improve in Capitalistic Societies

Another positive aspect of capitalism is that it is dependent upon healthy relationships. Every business owner knows that he must keep his customers happy or the customers will go somewhere else. So too the employees must be satisfied or they will not perform well. Businesses must pay their bills and treat people fairly if they want to stay in business. Nations doing commerce with other nations must maintain peace.

Therefore, capitalism provides an incentive to create and maintain good relationships. The business owner is motivated to inspire his or her employees to put on a smile. Businesses must constantly work at communicating and breaking down barriers. Nations must work together and secure each others' well-being. Big businesses, in particular, (except those which provide for military needs) depend on cooperation among nations and can only advance if nations are at peace with one another. Hence, capitalism is a powerful force to nurture peace among all people.

The resulting differences between capitalistic and socialistic societies are blatant. To get a small glimpse of this, simply travel to a socialistic country and try to purchase something at the local grocery store. Look into the eyes of the clerk at the checkout counter—if he will even give you eye contact. Next, travel to a big city in the U.S. and you will be amazed at the warm customer service. Certainly some of the friendliness is contrived, but even that breeds more friendliness which permeates and invigorates society.

72. People Need to Work, Struggle and Grow

Capitalism demands that people struggle to get ahead but diehard socialists think that struggle and competition are evil. In reality, the struggle is the process by which people grow in their ability to handle success. This is similar to how people build their muscles: if there is no resistance, muscles cannot develop. So also, if there is no struggle in life, people do not mature.

On the other hand, being given money without working for it produces an unhealthy lifestyle. It goes back to the passive, you-take-care-of-me, poverty mind-set. Welfare recipients often resent their benefactor. Communism produced masses of alcohol and drug addicted people as they were left without incentives to produce.

The best economic system is one which provides a structure in which people have the right to life, liberty and the pursuit of happiness. Individuals must be allowed to connect with their personal dreams and then work to fulfill those dreams.[27] That system is capitalism.

---

27 For further teaching on achieving success through pursuing your dreams read: John S. Garfield. *Desire to Destiny* (Kennewick, WA: Releasing Kings Publishing, 2007).

73. The Place of Government

So what do we want our government to do?

There are some responsibilities which can only be handled effectively by the government: tasks such as policing our cities and defending the nation. Government must also ensure property rights and freedom. It is for the benefit of all when government encourages the development of an infrastructure which facilitates business. Because unregulated capitalism can be abusive, government must also limit and prosecute unrighteous business dealings. It must protect the rights of individuals so that the successful do not oppress the poor. It must break up monopolies wherein competition is eliminated. It must disrupt huge corporations which attempt to control the markets unjustly. Government must ensure a well-balanced equilibrium between liberty and order.[28]

But government must not hinder the human spirit which most freely expresses itself in capitalism. Government must not hinder the entrepreneur and innovator. It must encourage progress by allowing those who excel to reap the rewards of their labor.

74. Socialistic Governments Are Oppressive

Both capitalistic and socialistic governments struggle for a balance between freedom and control of the population, but the more socialistic, the more controlling. This is because the more control the government has to govern the flow of goods and services, the more it can demand certain behaviors from the recipients. Over time this control grows stronger and stronger.

This is not only true in communistic societies, but even

---

28 For an excellent discussion of some other tasks best handled by the government, see: Charles Wheelan. *Naked Economics* (New York: W. W. Norton & Co., 2002).

in the U.S. every move toward socialism puts more power in the hands of the government. One example is with the educational system. The federal government gives large financial grants to schools but that money always comes with strings attached in the form of standards which must be met. The more money a specific school receives, the more control the federal government exercises. While the school benefits from the additional money, the teachers and administrators often resent their loss of freedom as the demands to meet federal standards increase.

Within the capitalistic economy it is the wealthy individuals and large corporations which can take advantage of the less fortunate, however, just laws can limit that oppression. In addition, businesses can be limited by competition, customer response and employee performance. In contrast, when government becomes the oppressor, it is more difficult to limit. Of course, welfare states such as those in Europe do have courts to provide checks and balances, but it is difficult to stop the ever-expanding governments and ever-increasing control.

75. The Current Move toward Socialism

At the present time many nations in the West are moving in the direction of socialism.[29]

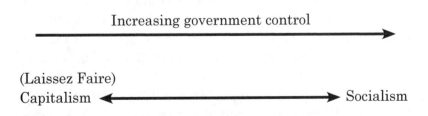

Increasing government control

(Laissez Faire)
Capitalism ←————————————→ Socialism

---

29 There are also socialistic nations like China and Russia which are becoming more capitalistic.

93

Here in the U.S. our current move toward socialism is very much the result of socialistic ideals being taught in our universities, creating a constant flow of young new socialists into leadership positions in society.

This concerns me as it concerns everyone who understands the energy released in a capitalistic economy and the detrimental effects of a socialistic economy. It is an especially important issue for Jews and Christians who understand that capitalism originated with God as He worked among His Old Testament people.

76. The Forces Driving Capitalism

Socialists try to sell the idea of socialism by putting capitalism in a very negative light. One of the most powerful images they use results from their criticism that the underlying forces that drive capitalism are greed and fear. When these are seen as the driving forces, it is easy to question whether anything good can ultimately come out of capitalism.

In reality, the primary forces driving capitalism are not greed and fear. To see this think of the average person going to work every Monday morning within a capitalistic society. What are his or her motivations? Of course, the accumulation of wealth is one motivation, but there are many others. Most parents go to work in order to provide for their family. They are motivated by love. Others go to work day after day because of a commitment to their vocation: doctors want to increase physical well-being, school teachers want to help children learn, soldiers hope to serve their country, social workers want to bring aid to the needy, preachers want to further the teachings of Christianity,... Still, many go to work simply because it is what people do. It is life. It is the way we live. They go to work out of habit. For the same reasons that people in socialistic societies go to work, people in capitalistic societies work.

However, in capitalistic societies there is the added motivation of challenge, excitement, fun and fulfillment. These added dimensions must not be minimized, for they are the pluses that allow capitalistic societies to advance far beyond socialistic ones. Millions of people are excited to go to work on Monday morning. They have discovered what they were born to do. Most Mondays they are eager to get to work because they find it fulfilling and meaningful.

Of course, there are *some people* in capitalistic societies who are motivated by greed. They may be trapped in a lifestyle which has a grip upon them from which they cannot escape. Jesus warned people about greed and the futility of hoarding great wealth. I can envision a few of those greedy capitalists when I think of various individuals on television programs which I have watched, but when I bring the vision closer to home and think of my successful capitalistic friends, I can't think of any one individual whom I would label as greedy. They each may have experienced short periods in their life when they were over-zealous, even work-alcoholics, but most, if not all of them have realized the vanity of such a lifestyle. They are actually the most generous people I know, financially supporting all kinds of family, community and church programs.

Envisioning a capitalistic society as a whole, a critical socialist can easily make a blanket judgment and condemn it as a greedy machine. But when we look at the individuals who make up that society, we realize that greed is not the primary driving force. As I said, many people in capitalistic societies go to work out of habit or a commitment to their vocation, but they are also motivated by love, excitement, challenge, fun and fulfillment.[30]

---

30 In his scholarly book, *The Protestant Ethic and the Spirit of Capitalism,* Max Weber presents his brilliant arguments and then dismisses the idea of greed being the driving force of capitalism, writing, "This naive conception of capitalism ought to be given up once and for all in the nursery school of cultural history."

77. Fear as a Driving Force

There are also *some people* in capitalistic societies who are motivated by fear—fear that they will not be able to eat or pay their mortgage, but I do not believe that is the primary motivation for most people. Everyone may at times experience passing thoughts and emotions of fear, especially during times of lack. But most people quickly learn that such motivations are non-productive, and hence, they cast them aside—they grow up—they realize that fear should not control their life.

On the other hand, some fear is okay. As the apostle Paul wrote, *"If anyone is not willing to work, then he is not to eat, either"* (II Thess. 3:10b). Fear of not eating can be a good motivation. If that is what it takes to motivate lazy people, then so be it. Socialistic societies which remove all fear by providing all needs are in error. They are undermining a fundamental God-given drive which motivates people to get out of bed and go to work.

So the socialistic idea that capitalism is driven by the evil forces of greed and fear is foolishness. It is socialistic societies which have a problem with motivation.

78. Should We Have a Classless Society?

Socialists are attempting to create a "classless society" in which all people share equally in all material possessions. They want no gap between the have and have not's. But if there was no gap, we would no longer be rewarding people for their wisdom and diligence. There should be some rich/poor gap because there is a wise-and-diligent/foolish-and-lazy gap.

The concept of a classless society reaches beyond financial provisions and extends into societal pressure to conform in many ways. This is immediately evident when a person visits a communist country and sees how no one wants to stand out in a crowd; everyone wears dull-colored clothing. Communistic countries encourage their citizens to see each other as "comrades," that is, as equals serving one another rather than serving self. Of course, there are positives in such servant attitudes, but on the negative side, individualism is squelched.

In working with various churches in ex-communistic countries I have seen how difficult it is to get individuals to rise up and lead. After three or four generations of everyone living under a value system of "equality" no one dares to stand up and be recognized. It is difficult to find a leader, because few people are capable of initiating new ideas or even speaking out their thoughts in front of a group.

Such incapacitation permeates socialistic societies. Yet it is so subtle that people within the system are unaware of its effect upon themselves. Without realizing it they allow themselves to act and live at a standard less than God intended.

79. Justice Versus Fairness

Capitalism promotes justice while socialism promotes fairness. Of course, I am using specific definitions of these words to make this point. Every socialist wants to see all people treated fairly in the sense that they all receive the same benefits including food, housing, education, salary and medical treatment. In contrast, capitalism distinguishes between fairness and justice, pointing out that justice rewards someone for their wisdom and diligence. It is unjust to give to a lazy person the same rewards that are given to a diligent person. Justice is a godly value, while fairness (as used here) is unjust.

80. The Modern Businessperson

Socialists who are antagonist toward capitalism often paint the modern capitalist as a selfish beast, always wanting more and caring little for employees or the environment. If that is the definition of a modern capitalist then I too am against capitalism.

However, a more realistic image of the modern capitalist can only be formed if we "put a face to it." Sit in a Chamber of Commerce meeting someday and you will meet business men and women who share high moral values. Capitalists are not faceless individuals who care for no one but themselves. Most of them live by high standards. They care about their community, employees and environment. Of course, there are a few jerks out there, but they are in the minority of successful businesspeople.

Surveys of business leaders indicate that most bosses do not like to fire employees.[31] Business owners are not mean, abusive individuals, discarding employees at their slightest whim. The vast majority of business owners care about their employees and families. Whenever financial pressures require them to release employees, they experience great anguish. Most carry the daily burden of keeping their businesses productive and their employees able to make a living. They *want* to provide jobs. They are trying to do the right thing.

When I put faces on capitalists, I think of some of my friends. None of those friends are hard-hearted or care only about themselves. Like I said earlier, they are among the most generous people I know. When I think of those individuals, I want to support capitalism because it allows wonderful people to be industrious, creative and generous.

---

31 Many such surveys have been done; one is mentioned on: http://www.jobbankusa.com/news/business_human_resources/opinions_advice_firing_people.html

Even now I am planning another trip to Africa. This time I will take ten business people with me. I know they will fall in love with my African friends. As a consequence, they will help finance the orphanage, schools and medical center which we now have under construction. We are also going because a local African Chamber of Commerce is hosting us. For three days they will gather together several hundred local business people and others who desire to start businesses, so we can encourage and advise them. I am doing this because I love my friends in Africa.

Summary

Socialism is increasing in the Western world, and this is very much the result of our educational system focusing the attention of students upon the past abuses and negatives of capitalism. Indeed there are some negatives in unrestrained capitalism, but history and modern experience reveal the greater evils of socialism.

Capitalism which is governed wisely and implemented with Godly values brings blessings. It brings to the poorer regions of the world hope and opportunities. It helps to provide peace, safety, roads, clean water, electricity, education and medical care. Capitalism allows development, progress, prosperity and cooperation. Throughout the world, capitalism, when properly governed, produces healthy relationships, healthy people and a healthy society.

Section V
A Revolution of
Compassionate Capitalism

In this last section I am going to discuss the wisdom, rightness and godliness of using some of our wealth to provide aid and care for the disadvantaged and oppressed among us. I will discuss the role of the individual, family, Church and government. Because the government's role is most in question, I will spend the largest portion of time dealing with its role in implementing compassionate capitalism.

81. The Role of the Individual

Jesus set the standard for His disciples by directing much of His attention toward the sick, downcast and poor. From the start He declared His purpose:

> *"The Spirit of the Lord is upon Me,*
> *Because He anointed Me to preach the gospel to*
> *   the poor.*
> *He has sent Me to proclaim release to the captives,*
> *And recovery of sight to the blind,*
> *To set free those who are oppressed."*
>
> (Luke 4:18)

The heart of Jesus is the heart of God. Those who honor Him as Lord, will value the things He valued and live as He lived. Jesus explained how He would reward His followers on judgment day:

> *"Then the King will say to those on His right,*
> *'Come, you who are blessed of my Father, inherit*

*the kingdom prepared for you from the founda-
tion of the world. For I was hungry, and you gave
Me something to eat; I was thirsty, and you gave
Me something to drink; I was a stranger, and you
invited me in; naked, and you clothed Me; I was
sick, and you visited Me; I was in prison, and you
came to Me.' "*

(Matt. 25:34-36)

Christians believe that one's eternal destiny will first of all
be determined by one's faith in Jesus Christ. But the apostle
James explained that one's faith will always be demonstrated
by righteous acts (James 2:14-26). We should not lose sight of
our eternal rewards:

*For we will all stand before the judgment seat of
God...So then each one of us will give an account
of himself to God.*

(Rom. 14:10-12)

Only a consciousness of eternity brings our present life into
proper focus. Only a consciousness of eternity will form a
foundation for how we should use our wealth today.

82. The Role of the Family

The family too must be involved in caring for the needy.
First and foremost they are responsible for their own members. Paul stated this most clearly:

*But if anyone does not provide for his own, and es-
pecially for those of his household, he has denied
the faith and is worse than an unbeliever.*

(I Tim. 5:8)

These words reveal the values held by the early Church. It is worth noting that the early Church consisted primarily of Jews who had received Jesus as Messiah. Their value system is the foundation of our Christian ethic.

83. The Role of the Church

The Church must also emulate the values of our Lord Jesus. Of course, there are many roles it must fulfill, but taking care of the needy should be a high priority.

In the book of Acts we read how the early Church was involved in helping the less fortunate. On Pentecost Day the Church was empowered by God's Spirit and Christians began selling their possessions and giving to anyone who had need (Acts 2:45). In a short time they established the position of deacon to provide food for the widows among them (Acts 6:1-6). The apostle Paul wrote instructions to his disciple Timothy as to how he should have the widows taken care of.

However, Paul told Timothy not to allow people to take advantage of the Church's generosity. He wrote that widows should not be provided for if they are able to provide for themselves or if they have family members who can care for them (I Tim. 5:3-16). The lesson is clear: the Church should be involved in caring for the needy, but only if the individual or family are not able to provide the necessary provisions.

84. The Role of Government

We have noted the Judeo-Christian value of the individual, family and Church being involved in caring for the needy. Now, we can consider the role of the government.

At this point some of my strict capitalist friends may close their ears to this discussion. They are convinced that the government has absolutely no business being involved in any social aid programs. I agree that our government should be limited in size and, therefore, in the role it takes in social work. However, there are some social programs which are best carried on by the government.

For example, the Child Protective Agency has the authority to remove abused children from one home and place them in a safe, loving environment. Of course, there are overly zealous social workers who make mistakes, but the government "bears the sword," and hence, has the authority to do certain things that the individual, family or Church cannot do.

Another social responsibility best carried out by the government is in making deadbeat fathers provide for their own children. There are too many men who have fathered children and then abandoned them (sometimes this applies to mothers). It would be great if the family and Church were involved in helping abandoned families, but the government can enforce a Judeo-Christian value by pursuing deadbeat fathers, confiscating some of their wages and using them to provide for their children.

I don't mind paying taxes that fund such social programs which are best carried on by the government.

85. Social Programs which Benefit Us All

The government should also be involved in some social programs which benefit us all. For example, one program provides anti-psychotic drugs to needy ex-convicts; I am grateful our government provides those drugs free of charge.

Our government also steps in to help out in incidents of national tragedies, such as floods, earthquakes and droughts. Sometimes these programs have been administered poorly with millions of dollars wasted, but still we need our government to be involved in some way. Without the government's involvement in such national tragedies, untold numbers of citizens would be devastated and large regions of our country would remain as unproductive as third-world countries. We need these programs, but we need more efficient management.

Society also benefits through government-funded programs which educate its citizens. If the government quit offering education, society's progress would slow dramatically and some areas would quickly deteriorate into harbors of crime, drugs and poverty. On the negative side, I am very concerned by how much our *federal* government has taken control of the education of our children, as it should be entirely in the hands of local governments and parents to whom local governments are held accountable. This is because God has delegated to parents—not the government—the authority to raise their own children.

86. Programs which Benefit the Oppressed

Beyond the social programs which require the sword to enforce and those which benefit us all, should the government be involved in other social programs? Let's consider programs specifically designed to offer aid to oppressed and disadvantaged people groups.

As a Christian I must offer some support for such programs, because there are examples of such government-sponsored programs in the Bible. For me, those examples set a precedent concerning what God wants for us.

For example, think of Nehemiah who was the cupbearer to King Artaxerxes. Nehemiah was a Jew who won the favor of the king and the king granted his wish for the Jews to be released from slavery. The king allowed the Jews to return to Jerusalem and rebuild the walls of their city. Further, the king sent army officers with Nehemiah and he ordered that the governors throughout the region give aid to the Jews (Neh. 2).

In the book of Esther we read how God gave favor to both Esther and her uncle Mordecai. As a result they were given positions next to King Ahasuerus, where they were able to obtain government favors for all of the Jews.

For another example, consider how Solomon's Temple in Jerusalem was destroyed, but Herod the governor of Judea funded its reconstruction.

We could list other government-funded programs from the Bible, but the point is that God was involved in raising certain individuals to obtain or give favor for oppressed people. This does not mean we should open the floodgates for every small group to obtain aid from the government. However, God does intervene in history in order to give relief to the oppressed. What God did in the past, He may do in our times. Jesus declared that He came *"To set free those who are oppressed."* Since this is God's heart, we should embrace it as our heart.

In accordance with this value, I must, in good conscious, give approval to some of the past social actions which my country has taken to benefit oppressed people. For example, after the Civil War, our U.S. government set aside land for slaves who had been freed. This was a government-sponsored program, which cost the nation money. I am glad my country took this action. It was right.

If I am willing to admit to any positive government-funded social programs in the past, then I should be open the possibility that there may be some positive actions taken in the future. I am not giving credence to every social action program that we have taken, nor do I think we should continue with all of the programs we have already established, but as a Christian who values the Bible, I am open to future programs which benefit oppressed or disadvantaged people.

87. Benevolent Social Programs?

Beyond the social programs mentioned, should the government be involved in benevolent programs which simply offer aid and care for its citizens? I am going to offer some support for a few more government-funded social programs, but first I need to post some warnings.

The first warning is sometimes accredited to the Scottish historian Sir Alex Fraser Tytler (1742-1813):

> *A democracy cannot exist as a permanent form of government. It can only exist until a majority of voters discover that they can vote themselves largess out of the public treasury.*[32]

Of course, the U.S. is a republic rather than a democracy, but the democratic element of our government allows the majority to secure the greatest benefits for themselves.

Another famous quotation adds to this:

> *Democracy is two wolves and a lamb voting on what to have for lunch. Liberty is a well-armed lamb contesting the vote.*[33]

This warning refers to the fighting and turmoil resulting from people being allowed access to government funding. When a government is involved in more than protecting its citizens, enforcing laws and building infrastructure to support progress, the coffers are open for a feeding frenzy. The strongest, most viscous and most organized will prevail. Many fight for the welfare of others, but some are carried on by greed.

---

[32] Even though this quotation is often accredited to Tytler, it cannot be verified as it does not appear in any of his published writings.

[33] This quotation is often accredited to Benjamin Franklin, but it cannot be verified as it does not appear in any of his published writings.

Today we see these dynamics as politicians, lobbyists and special interest groups spend millions of dollars and the majority of their energies fighting over available funds. Politicians gain support by gaining benefits for their constituents. Once the government offers its resources to care for its people, the battlefields are open and citizens will be at war with one another.

In addition to the wars waged once government funds are made available, consider those who must produce those funds.

> *The democracy will cease to exist when you take away from those who are willing to work and give to those who would not.*[34]

Margaret Thatcher stated it even stronger:

> *The problem with socialism is that eventually you run out of other people's money.*[35]

The more we move in the direction of socialism, the more we allow the angriest and most vocal to discourage and destroy the wise and diligent.

88. Will the Family and Church Do It?

Making government funding available to the masses opens Pandora's box, but we would be foolish to end all social aid to fellow-citizens who have needs. Please let me explain.

If the government suddenly ended all social work, millions of elderly would be abandoned. Homeless and mentally-handicapped people would wander the streets. Cripples

---

34 This statement is sometimes accredited to Thomas Jefferson, but it cannot be verified as it does not appear in any of his published writings.

35 http://en.wikiquote.org/wiki/Talk:Margaret_Thatcher

would be begging on the street corners. Unemployed families would starve and thievery would skyrocket. This is what is presently happening in countries where the government is not providing some care for the needy.

I wish this was not true. I wish our government did not have to offer social welfare. I wish the extended family and local churches fulfilled all of society's social needs. But the truth is that the family and Church have not done a good job in the past. Many families simply abandon their less fortunate relatives. The Church has always carried on some benevolent programs but there have always been huge gaps in services provided. The truth is that most churches can barely pay their own expenses let alone provide for the needy in their community.

I cannot emphasize this point enough, because some of my strict capitalistic friends continue holding to the myth that the family and Church would do all of the social service work if the government stayed out of it. Of course, we can encourage the family and Church to do more, but we also have to face reality: thinking that the family and Church are going to do it all is living in a fantasy world, and answers don't come from fantasies.

Therefore, I am going to offer some more support for government-funded social programs and critics may say that I am moving in the direction of the socialism. That may be true in one sense, because it requires the government to take on more social responsibility. But in another sense, it is not true because I am offering no support for the government owning, managing or controlling the country's means of production and distribution. I want people to be rewarded according to their labor, wisdom, experience and education. I believe in private ownership and free enterprise. But I also believe in compassionate capitalism. I want my government to be involved—in a limited way—in taking care of its less fortunate citizens.

In what way should the government be involved? We must answer this by addressing the issues from a practical basis. Who are the beneficiaries? How much will the programs cost? Who will pay? How will they affect society as a whole? Only if we have thought through these issues can we proceed with a sense of integrity.

89. Who Are the Beneficiaries?

A major obstacle in getting leaders to any kind of consensus concerning what, if any, social programs we should implement results from our differing perceptions concerning who will be the beneficiaries. When purist capitalists think of the beneficiaries they tend to envision a lazy 40-year-old man who is receiving welfare so he can spend his days smoking cigarettes, watching television and complaining about how hard life is. In contrast, socialists tend to envision the 80-year-old widow who has no children to help her, the mentally disturbed man walking the streets, or the single mother who was abandoned by her lazy 40-year-old husband. When thinking of health care programs, capitalists tend to envision the illegal alien who shows up at the local hospital emergency room expecting immediate care. In contrast, socialists tend to think that the beneficiary is a frail eight-year-old girl whose stomach is hurting but her mother cannot afford to take her in to see a doctor. With these different views of beneficiaries it is no wonder that no consensus can be reached when discussing how much we should help the needy.

Of course, the beneficiaries of government aid include all of the above mentioned individuals, but "contrary to popular opinion, most government benefits do not go to the poor; they go to the middle class in the form of Medicare and Social Security."[36] Of course, we can question the value and effectiveness of Medicare and Social Security, but it is important that we are dealing with truth when we discuss these issues.

Beyond the beneficiaries of Medicare and Social Security we have all types of individuals receiving social benefits. This includes all of the individuals mentioned above: widows with no family support, physically or mentally handicapped individuals, single mothers, children living under the poverty level and lazy 40-year-old men. Of course, there are many others, but this list includes the needy and the lazy.

Our government attempts to sort out the lazy, but there will always be mistakes made and some people will learn how to work the system to their own advantage. Furthermore, government is cumbersome, too big, too impersonal to do the work requiring personal contact with individuals. Policies and procedures replace decisions that need to be based on compassion and first-hand information. Too many individuals fall through the cracks while others take advantage of the system. The longer the programs are in operation the more complex and impersonal they become.

These are major arguments against the government taking on any social responsibilities of caring for its citizens.

90. Not All Social Programs Are Bad

However, we would be foolish to condemn the whole social benefit system. In spite of the flaws evident in our present social programs, anyone who has first-hand information about government-funded social programs knows that they are not completely heartless or ineffective. There are thousands of social workers who are compassionate and eager to help the

---

36 Charles Wheelan. *Naked Economics* (NY: W. W. Norton & Company, 2002). p. 59.

needy. The reason many give their lives to social work is because they love people and they believe in the system. Most are working long hours at low wages. Of course, there are some programs which are very wasteful and even detrimental, but there are also some which to me reveal the heart of God.

We must put a face to those social workers just like we earlier put a face to businesspeople. When I put a face to social workers I think of my son who has spent years helping elderly citizens obtain services so they can remain in their own homes as long a possible. I think of my sister who makes little more than minimum wage providing help to mentally-impaired adults. I think of a friend who works in a probation department helping ex-convicts get jobs and become contributing members of society. And I think of the social worker who helped me place my elderly father into a long-term Alzheimer's care facility. Of course, there are many others I can think of if I try, but these are the ones which immediately come to mind when I think of people working in government-financed social programs.

I can assure you that it is not just an impersonal machine funneling millions of dollars into the hands of lazy 40-year old men. If it was, then I too would be totally against it. But I have observed the system up close. It is personal. Compassionate people are touching real people with real needs.

91. Government Creates Dependency

If we are looking for problems with the government social aid programs, we could note how beneficiaries sometimes become dependent in the sense that they are increasingly unable to take care of themselves. Along with this dependency comes an expectation that something is owed to them. It is those dependents which capitalists most object to supporting.

To make this point, allow me to draw on my experience in working with the people of developing nations. With over 20 years traveling the world and helping needy people, I have learned how *not* to help people. If I present myself as a generous donor wanting to help, needy people will come out of the woodwork. Immediately my relationship with those people becomes distorted. They begin looking to me as their provider, their source of supply. Once that dynamic is set up in our relationship, I find it more difficult to work with the people in the sense of trying to teach them better ways to live. Rather than listening to my advice, they are distracted, hoping I will hurry up and finish talking so they can receive their handout. Furthermore, they stop looking to their previous avenues of provision and they stop developing those avenues. If and when I run out of money, they often express their disappointment and even anger toward me. Furthermore, they end up worse off than before I started giving aid, because their previous forms of support have been neglected and, hence, diminished.

One thing has become evident through the years: if I want to help someone in a developing nation, I help someone who is determined to succeed with or without my help. If I come alongside of someone who is already advancing by using what he or she already has available to them, then my help will amplify their efforts. On the other hand, if I help someone who is doing nothing except waiting around for someone to give them free aid, then my aid will only go a short distance and they will stop advancing as soon as I end my support.

Of course, I want to help everyone who is desperate and needs support just to stay alive. However, I have learned to only give significant aid to those who have vision and a drive to succeed. As Jesus said, *"For to everyone who has, more shall be given."* We can offer sustenance to the destitute, but we should only extend a generous hand to those who are trying to advance.

Still, I question who should be involved in giving such aid. Should the government? I will mention a few more negative aspects about the government's involvement in such programs, but then I want to redirect our attention to the role successful capitalists can have as free individuals helping the less fortunate.

92. Slowing the Successful Slows Society

A major drawback to government-funded social programs is that they are financially costly. The family and Church can take care of the needy much more economically because workers are often volunteers, food and supplies are often donated, and there is little overhead. Because money is limited and the family and Church will be using their own resources they will be careful distributing those resources. In contrast, the government will be more wasteful because people are never as careful when they are spending other people's money (that is, money raised through taxes).

Add onto this the fact that most of the cost will be placed on the backs of the successful. When the successful are slowed down, all of society slows down.

Too see this, compare successful capitalists to a herd of horses running across the open plain. They are free and fast-moving. When the government requires the capitalists to incorporate and license their businesses, it is comparable to putting bits into the mouths of the horses. As the capitalists are required to document every expenditure, the horses are reigned. As they are told how to do business, the horses are being directed where they can and cannot run. As the capitalists are taxed heavily, large weights are placed on the backs of the horses and if the weights are too heavy, they will never run again.

Of course, modern socialists think we are not putting enough on the backs of the successful, but we must consider what effect taxation and regulation is now having. The majority of new businesses which open in the U.S. fail within the first year. Many of those failures are simply due to the errors of the business owner, but it is also true that many would not have failed if government taxation[37] and regulation had been less. Every year there are thousands of business people closing their doors, and a large percentage will report that the reason is not because of a lack of business, but rather because the legal requirements imposed by the government are too excessive. When business owners need to spend more than 40 percent of their energy serving the government rather than producing what the business is designed to produce, the tendency is to give up and look for an easier way to make a living.

We need successful capitalists running ahead, bringing innovations, creating jobs for millions and propelling society forward. But to encourage them to do so, we must allow them to reap the benefits of their labors. We must not muzzle them while they work the fields.

93. The Overall Cost to Society

In addition to higher taxes on the wealthy, socialists are promoting universal health care, unemployment insurance, increased welfare, free and equal education benefits to all, minimum wage laws and a host of social programs. None of these things are evil in and of themselves, but we must consider the costs versus the benefits of each program. Plus, we need to consider the overall effects upon society.

---

37 The United States has one of the highest rates of taxation on corporations in the world; for the statistics see: www.taxfoundation.org/publications/show/23034.html

We know that every move toward socialism enlarges government and deposits within its hands more power to control people. The more that the government takes responsibility for, the less the individual will take responsibility for. With decreasing responsibility there is decreasing initiative. With decreasing initiative comes social stagnation and poverty.

Increasing government control

→

Active People	Passive People
Stimulating Initiative	Crushing Initiative
Rewarding Entrepreneurship	Penalizing Entrepreneurship
Elevating Human Dignity	Undermining Human Dignity
Creating Self-sufficiency	Creating Government Dependency
Empowering Humanity	Disabling Humanity
Activation of Society	Stagnation of Society
Creating Wealth	Engendering Poverty

(Laissez Faire) ←————————→ Socialism

I am concerned that we are moving too far in the direction of socialism.

94. God's Warning

My greatest concern comes as a result of the warning God gave to His Old Testament people about not allowing an overbearing government to take control. Through the prophet Samuel, God told the people that the more power a king is given, the more that king will demand and control them. Of course, non-Christians give no credence to the Bible and we Christians need to evaluate to what degree we should apply the Old Testament standards to our lives today, but at the very least we should consider God's warning seriously.

He was talking about the negative consequences of having a king rule over them. God warned the Hebrew people that a king would continually increase his demands until eventually *"He will take a tenth of your flocks and you yourselves will become his servants."* (I Sam. 8:17). Today in many capitalistic-turned-more-socialistic countries the government takes more than 50 per cent of the average person's income. That means more than 50 per cent of each day is spent serving the government and providing for the needs (and wants) of others. This sounds like the very thing God was warning His people not to allow.

Of course, it would be wrong to make a direct correspondence between the king/subject form of government and our modern-day circumstances. At least here in the U.S. we have a representative form of government with our representatives elected by the people. Therefore, we can consider God's warning to the Hebrews but we must take into account the differences between a king-ruled country and our democratic republic. Unlike a nation with a king, people can choose to delegate to the government certain responsibilities.

Still, the warning is for us. The more social programs which our government takes on, the more it grows and feeds on us. Because I take God's warning seriously, I want to keep our government small. Even if the government could do a better job at carrying certain social responsibilities, we may be wise to leave some of those responsibilities undone for the sake of keeping our government in check.

95. Compassion Exercised by Personal Choice

Finally, we can set the government completely aside and focus on the form of compassionate capitalism which offers all of the benefits and none of the negatives. That form entails acts of compassion which are carried on by the free choice of successful capitalists.

Perhaps our greatest example in modern times is Bill and Melinda Gates. Through their foundation, along with the help of Warren Buffet and others, they are bringing innovations in health and learning to the global community. They may or may not be Christians (I don't know), but what they are doing is expressing the heart of God in ways from which we should all learn.

When compassion is exercised by business people, it is free of the encumbrances of government. Business people are trained to accomplish the most with every dollar. Huge amounts are not consumed in administration. Funds do not come from the pockets of the unwilling. Business people are wise in how to invest money in projects that allow others to succeed, rather than enable them to become dependent and irresponsible. Money is not distributed to gain political favors. Nor do business people need to be credited with their acts of compassion to gain votes for future positions.

The heroes of compassionate capitalism are those who build a successful business and then use some of the profits to fund an orphanage in Africa or a grade school in Afghanistan. The real heroes are the medical professionals who take one month off each year and serve as medical missionaries in poverty-stricken regions of the world. Then there are also the lawyers who take on pro-bono cases for the abandoned mother and disabled man. Similarly, there are building contractors and farmers who travel to storm and earthquake devastated regions. There are even professionals who were successful enough to retire by the time they reached middle-age, but they continued working, using their most productive years to build wealth to be used to help widows start businesses or refugees return to their homes.

The best youth program to reduce future incarceration is not that which a politician has sponsored; rather it is the local grocery store manager who allows teenagers to work during the after school hours. The best program to help single mothers is not one which offers tax benefits and government aid; it is the one in which a caring neighbor fixes the wrecked automobile of the single mom. The best adult education program is not one which the government funds through our universities or trade schools; rather, it is the training that a businesswoman offers her employees so they can advance within her business.

It is not just business giants who are good at caring on programs of compassion. It is the woman who buys groceries for the widow down the street. It is the couple who take in foster children and love them as their own. And it is the neighborhood boy who mows the lawn of the disabled homeowner.

The greatest compassion heroes are not the socialists who try to force the government to provide more for the needy. The real heroes are the individual citizens who have worked hard applying the principles of capitalism and then use their wealth to tackle society's woes. These are the heroes of our modern world. These are the compassionate capitalists who make this world a better place.

96. Acts of Compassion Require Wealth

If we want more compassionate capitalists, we need more capitalists. Compassionate people need capital.

Consider Leo Tolstoy, the famous Russian author of *War and Peace*. He owned a huge estate that employed hundreds of workers. Tolstoy was a generous man, caring for the needs of the peasants. After becoming a serious Christian he read our Lord's Sermon on the Mount and then decided that he should sell everything and give the proceeds to the poor. Unfortunately, his estate came into the possession of greedy owners who mistreated the peasants. In their plight, the peasants cried out to Tolstoy to deliver them, but he was no longer in a position to help. Tolstoy had given up his position of influence and authority. As a result people suffered.

What is the lesson? Prosperous people can help others. Of course, there may be a few individuals whom God has called to a sacrificial life, owning little and spending their days in prayer. But the vast majority of God's people should work six days a week and be productive. The more successful they are, the more they will have the authority and power to influence this world in a positive way.

This applies at all levels. The medical doctor can only go on a medical missions trip if he makes enough money to take time off and finance the mission. A business woman can only offer advanced training for her employees if her business is advancing. The business man can only fund an orphanage in Africa if he is making a profit. And the neighborhood boy can only mow the lawn of the disabled homeowner if he has a lawn mower. People can not be compassionate capitalists unless they are first capitalists.

97. Compassionate Capitalists Are Abundant

A critic may respond by saying that there are not enough compassionate capitalists in capitalistic societies. I would respond by saying, "Open up your eyes and look around you! There are compassionate capitalists everywhere in capitalistic societies!"

Take for example, the giants of the Industrial Revolution,

Andrew Carnegie and John E. Rockefeller. Carnegie was said to be the wealthiest man in the U.S., but he shrank his estate by giving away the vast amount, funding among other things 25,000 public libraries. After Rockefeller rose to the top he divested over 500,000,000, funding such things as Baptist churches, medical schools and the Rockefeller Foundation dedicated "to promote the well-being of mankind throughout the world." Today there are thousands of such foundations. Individual philanthropic endeavors are multiplied millions of times over.

I find compassionate capitalists all around me. They are my friends. They are the people in my community who provide jobs for others and want to make a positive impact upon society. Of course, there are some selfish jerks in the business world, but there are also millions of people who want to accomplish something significant beyond themselves. It is a real driving force within each of them.

To accept this, you must believe in people. This is the bottom line. What do you believe about people? I have come to believe that God has created people in His image. Of course, we all sin. We all fall short. But there is still some God-given drive in humanity. Just as there is a drive to succeed and prosper, there is also a desire in most people to help others. When given a chance, people will sacrifice to help their neighbors.

On the other hand, there is an emptiness in a life spent only pleasing oneself. Most people realize this. Sooner or later they mature, they grow up, they discover what is important in life. They want to be compassionate with their wealth and they will be compassionate if given a chance.

98. Compassion Towards One's Descendants

Compassionate dispersal of accumulated wealth becomes especially important as people approach the end of their life.

Death is the great equalizer. No one leaves this world with a penny. As people get older they become ever more conscious of this fact.

Of course, wealth can be left in the hands of one's descendants. As Solomon wrote:

"A good man leaves an inheritance to his children's children"

Prov. 13:22a

As discussed earlier, it is a Judeo-Christian value to leave an inheritance.

But this value went hand-in-hand with the value of honoring one's parents. It was applied in a culture where children worked in the family business and learned to work side-by-side their father and mother.

...there is a man who has labored with wisdom, knowledge and skill, then he gives his legacy to one who has not labored with them. This too is vanity and a great evil.

(Eccl. 2:21)

Life reveals that children who have never learned how to work will not be able to handle large amounts of unearned money. It goes back to the slave-like-you-take-care-of-me mind-set. Only children who have learned the value of work should be entrusted with wealth and never more than they can handle wisely.

Unfortunately, many parents give gifts to their children in order to get love rather than because they love. Someone who gives a large amount of money to a child who has not learned how to work is likely to cause more damage than good. That is not love. That is not compassion. In many cases it is cruel.

It is best to help hard-working children and grandchildren get an education, start a business and/or buy a home.[38] Any inheritance money given beyond that should not be passed on until they are well on in years.[39] The writer of Proverbs tells us:

> *An inheritance gained hurriedly in the beginning*
> *Will not be blessed in the end.*
>
> (Prov. 20:21)

Recognizing the dangers of giving large amounts of unearned wealth to one's descendants leads successful capitalists to consider other ways to distribute their wealth.

99. Being a Follower of Jesus

How should the successful distribute their wealth?

Before we conclude this discussion, make no mistake that successful capitalists should be free to do what they desire to do. Furthermore, God is not asking people to live so frugally that they fail to experience His blessings. In other words, He wants His children to enjoy the fruit of their own labors.

> *There is nothing better for a man than to eat and*
> *drink and tell himself that his labor is good. This*
> *also I have seen is from the hand of God.*
>
> (Eccl. 2:24)

After enjoying the blessings of this abundant earth, the successful capitalists are still left in a position of needing to

---

38 This is often done by setting up a trust which releases some money around age 18 to pay for education, some more at age 30 to help buy a home, and some around age 40 to help buy or build a business.

39 I suggest in their 50's (or 40's if they are very financially responsible).

distribute that which they cannot take with them beyond the grave. After giving to one's descendants that which they can handle, what should be done?

If you are trying to follow Jesus, you ought to consider what He would have you do. His will is always summed up in His words, *"Love God with your whole heart and your neighbor as yourself."* Follow this and you will do His will. Furthermore, you can ask God. He still answers prayer and guides those who are willing to follow Him.

100. Joining a Cultural Revolution

For society to embrace these Judeo-Christian values we need a cultural revolution. Too many have lost sight of the purpose for life. Our present society has hidden its head in the sand and ignored the coming day when we individually stand before the Great Judge of all humanity.

Because we have lost our way, we have become trapped in consumerism. We are slaves to the government and to ourselves. We work a few hours each day making money to pay taxes, but we work the rest of the day so we can surround ourselves with material possessions. Our goal is to work until we have achieved comfort and personal success. Then we shut off our power switch and begin to coast in life. We have no more drive for innovation, investments and the creation of wealth, because our goals were never to help our neighbors or solve society's woes. From start to finish our goals were only to help ourselves and our loved ones. We are slaves to our own needs and pleasures.

However, we do not have to be slaves. You and I can be free. We can prosper and use our prosperity to impact this world. You and I can live as we were created to live—free, industrious, entrepreneurial and compassionate. We can re-prioritize our goals. We can live a life that matters.

Furthermore, we can be part of a cultural revolution—a revolution that calls our fellow citizens to succeed for a purpose beyond themselves. We can embrace a lifestyle of generosity that exudes energy and becomes contagious. We can be the heroes of this generation.

Then we can teach these values to our children. In the same way that our children have been taught the values of environmental concern, so they can be taught to orient their lives toward solving society's woes. We can point them in the direction of success and compassion. They can be the heroes of the next generation.

The Church must rise up and lift the standard of Jesus Christ, directing His followers to embrace a lifestyle oriented toward lifting the downtrodden and oppressed. We must speak against greed and selfishness. We must warn of the deceitfulness of riches. We must be Christian.

At the same time we can mold our government. We have a choice. We can form a government which carries all responsibility for the care of its citizens, hence producing passive dependents. Or we can form a government which opens the doors for free people to embrace life and rise to the challenges surrounding them. We can build our society the way we want to build it.

My vote is for compassionate capitalism. I want the freedom to impact my world. I want the opportunity to be a blessing to every family on earth. This is the way God created us to live.

Summary

Compassionate capitalism is built on the foundation of private ownership and free enterprise, but some of the resulting prosperity must be used for social concerns. Some social programs are best carried on by the government. Those programs should be constantly evaluated and reshaped. We must be ever-conscious of the benefits versus the costs. We must also protect our economic system from being destroyed by an overbearing government.

Government can help but it is not the sole answer to society's woes. We need the family and Church to do their part. We also need successful capitalists to tackle the problems facing us.

For this to happen we must cast off the grip of selfishness. We must live as free individuals with a zeal to change the world around us. We must take full advantage of the capitalistic economic system which God has given to us. We must live as givers, not takers, as free people, not slaves to ourselves.

Conclusion

Capitalism is part of the Judeo-Christian ethic. However, the form of capitalism which God developed among the Hebrew people was not entirely free-market capitalism. God required the Hebrews to make provisions for the widows, orphans, poor, aliens and other needy. Caring for one's parents was also a strong cultural value. These values were not enforced by the government but the people believed they must serve God corporately, hence they kept each other accountable.

The New Testament reaffirms the fundamental principles of capitalism but it also offers cautions concerning the unrestrained pursuit of wealth. Jesus described a coming judgment day when every person will give an account for what they have done. A central basis of that judgment will be how we cared for the poor, the stranger, the sick and the imprisoned (Matt. 25:34-36). We should also note how our Lord Jesus and the apostle Paul warned of the deceitfulness of riches and the futility of hoarding great wealth.

History also offers us lessons concerning how we should handle wealth. Capitalism is the economic system which allowed a middle class to arise and society as a whole to advance and prosper. It was the gradual triumph of the Judeo-Christian ethic throughout Europe which led to capitalism displacing the cruel and oppressive economic systems of the Greek and Roman empires. However, capitalism with no restrictions led to abuses, especially evident during the period of Western colonization and industrialization. Throughout those periods it was Christian leaders who led in the establishment of individual rights, including the protection of children, limitations on labor, and care for the elderly and infirm. We should be grateful for many of those steps which tempered capitalism.

Compassionate Capitalism: A Judeo-Christian Value

Learning from the past and from the teachings of Scripture, Christians should work for and defend the economic system which releases the human spirit and produces abundance. This will be a battle because many leaders in our modern educational institutions are pro-socialism and anti-Christian. But capitalism is worth fighting for. It is even worth defending against an ever-growing government.

We need capitalism but we need it applied with compassion. The wisdom of compassionate capitalism leads us to delegate some social responsibilities to the government, but the most effective social programs will always be carried on by the family, Church and individuals who are successful at applying the principles of capitalism. Knowing this, we should cultivate a society which values free individuals impacting and affecting society for the benefit of all.

Recommended Reading

If this book has been helpful, you will also want to read the following two books.

Releasing Kings into the Marketplace for Ministry

Co-authored by
John Garfield and Harold R. Eberle

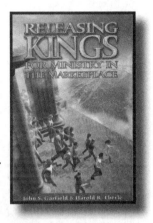

"Kings" is what we call Christian leaders who have embraced the call of God upon their life to work in the marketplace and from that position transform society. This book explains how marketplace ministry will operate in concert with local churches and pastors. It provides a Scriptural basis for the expansion of the Kingdom of God into all areas of society. It paints a picture of kings who are naturally competitive, creative, and decisive—who are being used to fulfill the Great Commission.

Desire to Destiny

Seven Keys to Your Marketplace Ministry

This is a sequel to the book described above. Written by John Garfield, it is aimed to bless the nations by releasing an army of kings, having a mission to change cultures with the Gospel of life more abundantly . . . impart the message, make the money, do the mission, and make more disciples that will make a difference.

Christianity Unshackled

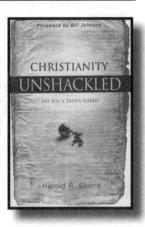

Most Christians in the Western world have no idea how profoundly their beliefs have been influenced by their culture. What would Christianity be like, if it was separated from Western thought? After untangling the Western traditions of the last 2,000 years of Church history, Harold R. Eberle offers a Christian worldview that is clear, concise, and liberating. This will shake you to the core and then leave you standing on a firm foundation!

God's Leaders for Tomorrow's World
(Revised/expanded edition)

You sense the call to leadership, but questions persist: "Does God want me to rise up? Do I truly know where to lead? Is this pride? How can I influence people?" Through an understanding of leadership dynamics, learn how to develop godly charisma. Confusion will melt into order when you see the God-ordained lines of authority. Fear of leadership will change to confidence as you learn to handle power struggles. It is time to move into your "metron," that is, your God-given sphere of authority.

Two Become One
(Second edition)
Releasing God's Power for Romance, Sexual Freedom and Blessings in Marriage

The keys to a thrilling, passionate, and fulfilling marriage can be yours if you want them. Kindle afresh the "buzz of love." Find out how to make God's law of binding forces work for you rather than against you. This book is of great benefit to pastors, counselors, young singles, divorces, and especially married people. Couples are encouraged to read it together.

Who Is God?

Challenging the traditional Western view of God, Harold R. Eberle presents God as a Covenant-maker, Lover, and Father. Depending on Scripture, God is shown to be in a vulnerable, open, and cooperative relationship with His people. This book is both unsettling and enlightening—revolutionary to most readers—considered by many to be Harold's most important contribution to the Body of Christ.

Precious In His Sight
A Fresh Look at the Nature of Humanity

During the Fourth Century Augustine taught about the nature of humanity using as his key Scripture a verse which had been mistranslated. Since that time the Church has embraced a false concept of humanity which has negatively influenced every area of Christianity. It is time for Christians to come out of darkness! This book has implications upon our understanding of sin, salvation, Who God is, evangelism, and how we can live the daily victorious lifestyle.

The Spiritual, Mystical, and Supernatural

The first five volumes of Harold R. Eberle's series of books entitled, *Spiritual Realities,* have been condensed into this one volume, 372 pages in length. Topics are addressed such as how the spiritual and natural worlds are related, angelic and demonic manifestations, signs and wonders, miracles and healing, the anointing, good versus evil spiritual practices, how people are created by God to access the spiritual realm, how the spirits of people interact, how people sense things in the spirit realm, and much more.

Other Books by Harold R. Eberle

Victorious Eschatology
A Partial Preterist View
Co-authored by
Harold R. Eberle and Martin Trench

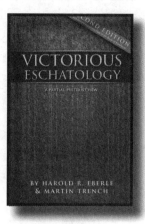

Here it is—a biblically-based, optimistic view of the future. Along with a historical perspective, this book offers a clear understanding of Matthew 24, the book of Revelation, and other key passages about the events to precede the return of Jesus Christ. Satan is not going to take over this world. Jesus Christ is Lord and He will reign until every enemy is put under His feet!

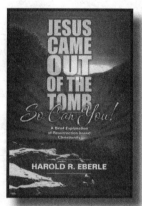

Jesus Came Out of the Tomb...So Can You!
A Brief Explanation of Resurrection-based Christianity

Forgiveness of sins is at the cross. Power over sin is in the resurrection and ascension. Unfortunately, too many Christians have only benefited from the death of Jesus and not His life. If God raised Jesus from the tomb in power and glory, then we can experience that resurrection power. If God raised Jesus into heaven, and us with Him, then we can live in His victory!